بسم الله الـ حمن الرحيم

ABOUT THE AUTHOR

Under the pen name HARUN YAHYA, the author has published many books on political and faith-related issues. An important body of his work deals with the materialistic world view and the impact of it in world history and politics. (The pen-name is formed from the names 'Harun' [Aaron] and 'Yahya' [John] in the esteemed memory of the two Prophets who struggled against infidelity.)

His works include The Secret Hand in Bosnia, Behind the Scenes of Terrorism, Israel's Kurdish Card, A National Strategy for Turkey, Solution The Morals of the Qur'an, Darwin's Antagonism Against the Turks, Articles 1, Articles 2, The Evolution Deceit, Perished Nations, The Prophet Musa, The Golden Age, God's Artistry in Colour, Glory is Everywhere, The Truth of the Life of This World, Confessions of Evolutionists, The Blunders of Evolutionists 1, The Blunders of Evolutionists 2, The Dark Magic of Darwinism, The Religion of Darwinism, The Qur'an Leads the Way to Science, The Real Origin of Life, The Consciousness of the Cell, The Creation of the Universe, Miracles of the Qur'an, The Design in Nature, Self-Sacrifice and Intelligent Behaviour Models in Animals, Eternity Has Already Begun, Children Darwin Was Lying!, The End of Darwinism, Deep Thinking, Timelessness and the Reality of Fate, Never Plead Ignorance, The Secrets of DNA, The Miracle of the Atom, The Miracle in the Cell, The Miracle of the Immune System, The Miracle in the Eye, The Creation Miracle in Plants, The Miracle in the Spider, The Miracle in the Ant, The Miracle in the Gnat, The Miracle in the Honeybee, The Miracle of Seed, The Miracle in the Termite, The Miracle of the Human Body, The Miracle of Man's Creation, Realities 1.

Among his booklets are The Mystery of the Atom, The Collapse of the Theory of Evolution: The Fact of Creation, The Collapse of Materialism, The End of Materialism, The Blunders of Evolutionists 1, The Blunders of Evolutionists 2, The Microbiological Collapse of Evolution, The Fact of Creation, The Collapse of the Theory of Evolution in 20 Questions, The Biggest Deception in the History of Biology: Darwinism.

The author's other works on Quranic topics include: Ever Thought About the Truth?, Devoted to God, Abandoning the Society of Ignorance, Paradise, The Theory of Evolution, The Moral Values of the Qur'an, Knowledge of the Qur'an, Qur'an Index, Emigrating for the Cause of God, The Character of Hypocrites in the Qur'an, The Secrets of the Hypocrite, The Names of God, Communicating the Message and Disputing in the Qur'an, The Basic Concepts in the Qur'an, Answers from the Qur'an, Death Resurrection Hell, The Struggle of the Messengers, The Avowed Enemy of Man: Satan, Idolatry, The Religion of the Ignorant, The Arrogance of Satan, Prayer in the Qur'an, The Importance of Conscience in the Qur'an, The Day of Resurrection, Never Forget, Disregarded Judgements of the Qur'an, Human Characters in the Society of Ignorance, The Importance of Patience in the Qur'an, General Information from the Qur'an, Quick Grasp of Faith 1-2-3, The Crude Reasoning of Disbelief, The Mature Faith, Before You Regret, Our Messengers Say, The Mercy of Believers, The Fear of God, The Nightmare of Disbelief, Prophet Isa Will Come, Beauties Presented by the Qur'an for Life, Bouquet of the Beauties of God 1-2-3-4, The Iniquity Called "Mockery", The Secret of the Test, The True Wisdom According to the Qur'an, The Struggle with the Religion of Irreligion, The School of Yusuf, The Alliance of the Good, Slanders Spread Against Muslims Throughout History, The Importance of Following the Good Word, Why Do You Deceive Yourself?, Islam: The Religion of Ease, Enthusiasm and Vigor in the Qur'an, Seeing Good in Everything, How does the Unwise Interpret the Qur'an?, Some Secrets of the Qur'an, The Courage of Believers, Being Hopeful in the Qur'an, Justice and Tolerance in the Qur'an

THE DISASTERS DARWINISM BROUGHT TO HUMANITY

TO THE READER

The reason why a special chapter is assigned to the collapse of the theory of evolution is that this theory constitutes the basis of all anti-spiritual philosophies. Since Darwinism rejects the fact of creation, and therefore the existence of God, during the last 140 years it has caused many people to abandon their faith or fall into doubt. Therefore, showing that this theory is a deception is a very important duty, which is strongly related to the religion. It is imperative that this important service be rendered to everyone. Some of our readers may find the chance to read only one of our books. Therefore, we think it appropriate to spare a chapter for a summary of this subject.

In all the books by the author, faith-related issues are explained in the light of the Qur'anic verses and people are invited to learn God's words and to live by them. All the subjects that concern God's verses are explained in such a way as to leave no room for doubt or question marks in the reader's mind. The sincere, plain and fluent style employed ensures that everyone of every age and from every social group can easily understand the books. This effective and lucid narrative makes it possible to read them in a single sitting. Even those who rigorously reject spirituality are influenced by the facts recounted in these books and cannot refute the truthfulness of their contents.

This book and all the other works of the author can be read individually or discussed in a group at a time of conversation. Those readers who are willing to profit from the books will find discussion very useful in the sense that they will be able to relate their own reflections and experiences to one another.

In addition, it will be a great service to the religion to contribute to the presentation and reading of these books, which are written solely for the good pleasure of God. All the books of the author are extremely convincing. For this reason, for those who want to communicate the religion to other people, one of the most effective methods is to encourage them to read these books.

It is hoped that the reader will take time to look through the review of other books on the final pages of the book, and appreciate the rich source of material on faith-related issues, which are very useful
and a pleasure to read.

In these books, you will not find, as in some other books, the personal views of the author, explanations based on dubious sources, styles that are unobservant of the respect and reverence due to sacred subjects, nor hopeless, doubt-creating, and pessimistic accounts that create deviations in the heart.

THE DISASTERS DARWINISM BROUGHT TO HUMANITY

HARUN YAHYA

Title: The Disasters Darwinism Brought To Humanity
Author: Harun Yahya
Translated by: Carl Rossini

Copyright: All rights reserved
Printed: 2001
Printing supervised by: M.R.Attique
Printed at : Toronto – Canada

First Published by Vural Yayıncılık, İstanbul, Turkey in October 2000

{C} Al-Attique Publishers Inc. Canada 2001
ISBN 1-894264-44-4

Published by: Al-Attique Publishers Inc.Canada
65-Treverton Drive Tel: (416) 615-1222
Scarborough Ont. Fax: (416) 615-0375
M1K 3S5 CANADA
E-mail: quran@istar.ca Website: www.al-attique.com
E-mail: al-attique@al-attique.com

REPRESENTATIVE IN USA
Islamic Education & Media
730 East 10th street, C.F,
Brooklyn, NY 11230
T+F: (718) 421-5428

DISTRIBUTOR IN SAUDI ARABIA
Dar-Al-Hadyan Publishers & Distributors
P/O Box No : 15031
Al-Riyadh:11444
T+F (966) 1-463-1685

Branch in Pakistan:
89 Qamer st People Colony
Shahdara Lahore
T+F : 9242-791-1678

Website: www.harunyahya.org - www.harunyahya.com
www.harunyahya.net email: info@harunyahya.org

CONTENTS

INTRODUCTION: THE BRINGERS OF PAIN TO THE 20TH CENTURY — 8

A SHORT HISTORY OF DARWINISM — 12

DARWIN'S RACISM AND COLONIALISM — 26

THE TERRIBLE ALLIANCE BETWEEN DARWIN AND FASCISM — 56

DARWINISM, THE SOURCE OF COMMUNIST SAVAGERY — 98

CAPITALISM AND THE FIGHT FOR SURVIVAL IN THE ECONOMY — 146

THE MORAL COLLAPSE BROUGHT ABOUT BY DARWINISM — 158

CONCLUSION: THE SWAMP OF DARWINISM MUST BE DRAINED — 166

APPENDIX: THE MISCONCEPTION OF EVOLUTION — 169

THE BRINGERS OF PAIN TO THE 20TH CENTURY

The 20th century, which we have just left behind us, was a century of war and conflict, leading to disasters, pain, massacres, poverty, and enormous destruction. Millions of people were killed, massacred, abandoned to hunger and death, and left without home or shelter, protection, or support. And all for nothing: in the name of serving deviant ideologies. Millions were left exposed to inhuman treatment that not even animals should be allowed to suffer. On nearly every occasion there were despots' and dictators' signatures beneath all the suffering and disasters: Stalin, Lenin, Trotsky, Mao, Pol Pot, Hitler, Mussolini, Franco… While some of these men shared the same ideology, others were enemies to the death. For the simple reason that their ideologies were opposed to each other, they dragged societies into conflict and turned brother against brother, having them start wars, throw bombs, burn and destroy cars, homes, and shops, and hold riotous demonstrations. Putting weapons in their hands, they had them pitilessly beat the young, the old, men, women, and children to death or stand them against a wall and shoot them… They were ruthless enough to hold a gun to a person's head and, looking into his eyes, kill him, and crush his head with their feet, just because he supported another idea. They ejected people from their homes, whether women, children, or the elderly…

That is a short resume of the nightmares of the 20th century that we have just emerged from: people who supported conflicting ideas and who drowned mankind in pain and blood in the name of supporting these ideologies.

Fascism and Communism come at the head of the ideologies that caused mankind to suffer those dark days. These are seen as enemies, as ideas that tried to destroy each other. In actual fact, there is a most interesting truth here: for these ideologies were nourished by a single ideological source, drew strength and support from that source, and, thanks to that source, were able to draw societies to their side. At first sight, this source has never drawn any attention, has always remained behind the scenes up until now, and has always shown people its innocent-looking face. That source is the materialist philosophy, and **DARWINISM**, the state of that philosophy as adapted to nature.

Darwinism emerged in the 19th century as the restating of a myth, dating back to the Sumerians and Ancient Greece, by the amateur biologist Charles Darwin, and has since then formed the fundamental idea behind all the ideologies that have been harmful to mankind. Wearing a so-called scientific mask, it allowed these ideologies and their supporters' practical measures to win a false legitimacy.

By means of this false legitimacy the theory of evolution soon left the fields of knowledge of biology and palaeontology and began to comment on fields from human relations to history, and to influence fields from politics to social life. Because some particular claims of Darwinism supported several currents of thought which began to come into motion and take shape in the 19th century, it gained wide support from these circles. In particular, people began trying to apply the idea that there is a "fight for survival" among living creatures in nature, and as a result, the idea that "the strong survive, the others are defeated and disappear" began to be applied to human thought and behaviour. When Darwinism's claim that nature was a place of struggle and conflict began to be applied to human beings and societies, Hitler's deviation of building a master race, Marx's claim that "the history of mankind is the history of class struggle," capitalism's provision for the "strong growing even stronger at the expense of the weak," the colonisation of third world countries by such imperialist nations as Britain and their suffering inhuman treatment, together with the fact that coloured people still face racist attacks and discrimination, all found some kind of justification.

Despite his being an evolutionist, Robert Wright, the author of the book *The Moral Animal* summarises the disasters that the theory of evolution has brought to the history of mankind in this way:

> Evolutionary theory, after all, has a long and largely sordid history of application to human affairs. **After being mingled with political philosophy around the turn of the century to form the vague ideology known as "social Darwinism," it played into the hands of racists, fascists, and the most heartless sort of capitalists.**[1]

As will be seen in this book and from the evidence it contains, Darwinism is not just a theory which attempts to explain the origin of life and which is restricted to the field of scientific knowledge. Darwinism is a dogma still stubbornly defended by the supporters of certain ideologies, despite the fact that it has been proven totally invalid from the scientific point of view. In our day many scientists, politicians and men of ideas, whether aware or not of Darwinism's dark face, lend their support to this dogma.

If everyone comes to know the scientific invalidity of this theory, which acts as an inspiration for cruel dictators, and ruthless, inhuman, and self-centred mentalities and currents of thought, that will spell the end of these harmful ideologies. Those who do and systematise evil will be unable to defend themselves by saying, "But this is a law of nature." They will have no more so-called scientific backing for their self-centred, selfish, and pitiless world view.

Once the idea of Darwinism, the root of harmful ideologies, is finally overturned, only one truth will remain. That is the truth that all human beings and the universe itself were created by Allah (God). People who understand this will also realise that the only reality and the only truth are in the holy book He sent down to us. When a large majority of people come to realise this truth, the pains, troubles, massacres, disasters, injustices, and poverty in the world will be replaced by enlightenment, openness, wealth, plenty, health and abundance. For this, every false idea harmful to humanity must be conquered and left to rot by the holy idea which will bring beauty to mankind. To reply to stones by throwing others, to answer blows with blows, to answer the aggressor with more aggression is not a solution. The solution is to bring down the ideas of those who do these things and to explain, patiently and kindly, the one truth with which they must replace them.

The aim in writing this book is to show those who defend Darwinism without seeing its dark face, knowingly or unknowingly, what it is they are actually supporting, and to explain what their responsibility will be as long as they pretend not to see the truth of it. Another aim is to warn those who do not believe in Darwinism, but who also do not see Darwinism as a threat to humanity.

PART 1

A SHORT HISTORY OF DARWINIS[M]

Before we turn to the pain and disasters that Darwinism has brought to the world, let us take a brief look at its history. Many people believe the theory of evolution, first put forward by Charles Darwin, to be a theory based on firm scientific evidence, observation and experiment. Whereas, as the originator of the theory of evolution is not Darwin, so the source of the theory is not scientific proof.

At one period in Mesopotamia, when idol-worshipping religions had hegemony, superstitions and myths regarding the roots of life and the universe abounded: one of these was the belief "evolution." According to the Enuma-Elish epic, which dates back to the Sumerians, there was a raging flood, and from this the gods called Lahmu and Lahamu suddenly emerged. According to the superstition, these idols first created themselves and then, becoming universal, formed other matter and living creatures. In other words, according to Sumerian myth, life suddenly came into being from the non-living watery chaos, evolved and developed.

We can see that this belief shows a close accordance with the theory of evolution's claim that "living things developed and evolved from non-living things." From this we can see that the idea of evolution does not belong to Darwin, but originally to Sumerian idol-worshippers.

Later, the myth of evolution found more space to live in another idol-worshipping civilisation, Ancient Greece. Ancient Greek materialist philosophers counted matter as the only thing which existed. They turned to the myth of evolution, an inheritance from the Sumerians, to explain how living things came about. In this way, materialist philosophy and the myth of evolution came together in Ancient Greece. From there it was carried to the culture of Rome.

A picture depicting the Sumerian water god. Just like the Sumerians, Darwinists believe that life emerged by coincidence from water. In other words, they see water as a god which created life.

These two concepts, each a myth belonging to idol-worshipping cultures, appeared in the modern world in the 18th century. Some European thinkers who studied ancient Greek sources took a liking to materialism. The common feature of these thinkers was that they were opponents of religion.

In this environment the first person to take the theory of evolution on in a detailed way was the French biologist Jean Baptiste Lamarck. In his theory, which would later be understood to be false, Lamarck proposed that all living creatures evolved from one another by small changes throughout their lives. One person who repeated Lamarck's claims, in a slightly different way, was Charles Darwin.

Darwin put forward this theory in his book *The Origin of Species*, which he published in England in 1859. In this book, the myth of evolution, which had come down from ancient Sumer, was put forward in some detail. He claimed that all species of living creatures came from one ancestor, born by chance in the water, and that they had grown different from one another by small changes which came about by coincidence.

This claim of Darwin's did not win much general acceptance from the men of science of his time. Fossil experts in particular were aware that Darwin's claim was nothing but the product of a fantasy. But despite this

Like idol-worshipping societies, Darwinists believe that life emerged by coincidence in water as a result of natural effects. According to this nonsensical claim, the unconscious atoms in the "primitive soup" in the picture joined together and decided to form living creatures.

Darwin's theory began to win more support from different circles as time passed. Because Darwin and his theory provided the missing foundation for the forces ruling in the 19th century.

The Reason for the Acceptance of Darwinism is Ideological

In the period when Darwin published his book *The Origin of Species* and put forward his theory of evolution, science was very backward. For example, the cell, which is today known to possess a most complicated system, was only visible as a blot through the simple microscopes in use at the time. For this reason Darwin saw no problem in claiming that life came about by chance from non-living material.

In the same way, the insufficiency of the fossil record at that time made it possible for it to be claimed that living creatures had come about from each other by minute changes. Whereas today, it is certain that the fossil record, as we explained a short while above, offers not one piece of evidence to support Darwin's claim that living creatures had come about by developing from one another. Up until recently, evolutionists used to try to get over the dilemma facing them by saying, "It will be found one day in the future." But they are now in the position of being unable to hide behind this explanation. (For detailed information see Chapter "The Misconception of Evolution")

Compared to today, the microscopes available in the 19th century were quite primitive and, as in the picture, could only view cells as blots.

Whatever the case, there was no change in the Darwinists' attachment to the theory of evolution. Supporters of Darwin have come down to our day by handing their faithfulness to Darwin on to one another like an inheritance for the last 150 years.

All right, what is the reason for Darwinism, despite the fact that its scientific invalidity is now openly apparent, appealing to certain circles, and for heavy propaganda being made regarding it?

The most defining feature of Darwin's theory is its denial of the existence of a Creator. According to the theory of evolution, life formed itself, by coincidence, from innate matter. This claim of Darwin provided a false scientific support for all atheist philosophies, beginning with mate-

Charles Darwin

rialist philosophy. Because up until the 19th century the great majority of men of science looked at science as a method of learning and discovering what God had created. Because this belief was widespread, atheist and materialist philosophies were unable to find suitable ground in which to develop. But by denying the existence of a Creator and forming an illusory support for atheist and materialist belief, the theory of evolution was a wonderful opportunity for them. For this reason they both identified with Darwinism and adapted the theory to their own ideologies.

Beside Darwinism's denial of the existence of God, another claim emerged to support 19th century materialistic ideologies: "The development of living creatures is linked to the struggle for life in nature. This struggle goes to the strongest. The weak are condemned to defeat and extinction."

Darwinism's co-operation with ideologies which have brought pain and disaster to the world is clearly revealed in this point.

Social Darwinism: The Adaptation of the Law of the Jungle to Human Behaviour

One of the most important claims of the theory of evolution is its basing the development of living creatures on the "fight for survival" in nature. According to Darwin, in nature there is a pitiless fight for survival, an eternal conflict. The strong always overcome the weak, and this makes development possible. The subtitle of the book *The Origin of Species* summed up this point of view. *"The Origin of Species by Means of Natural Selection or the Preservation of Favoured Races in the Struggle for Life"*.

The source of Darwin's inspiration on this matter was the English economist Thomas Malthus's book *An Essay on the Principle of Population*. This book indicated that a rather dark future awaited mankind. Malthus had calculated that left to itself, the human population would increase at enormous speed. The numbers would double every 25 years. However, food supplies would in no way increase at the same rate. In this event, mankind faced the permanent danger of starvation. The forces keeping population under control were disasters, such as war, famine, and disease. In short, in order for some people to live, it was necessary for others to die. Existence meant "permanent war."

Darwin declares that it was Malthus's book which made him think about the struggle for existence:

> In October, 1838, that is, fifteen months after I had begun my systematic inquiry, I happened to read for amusement Malthus on population, and being well prepared to appreciate the struggle for existence which everywhere goes on from long continuous observation of the habits of animals and plants, it at once struck me that under these circumstances favourable variations would tend to be preserved and unfavourable ones to be destroyed. The result of this would be the formation of new species. Here, then, I had at last got a theory by which to work.[2]

In the 19th century Malthus's ideas had been adopted by quite a wide public. Upper-class European intellectuals in particular supported Malthus's ideas. The importance that 19th century Europe gave to Malthus's ideas on population is put across in the article *The Scientific Background of the Nazi "Race Purification" Programme*:

> In the opening half of the nineteenth century, throughout Europe, members of the ruling classes gathered to discuss the newly discovered "Population problem" and to devise ways of implementing the Malthusian mandate, to increase the mortality rate of the poor: "Instead of recommending cleanliness to the poor, we should encourage contrary habits. In our towns we should make the streets narrower, crowd more people into the houses, and court the return of the plague. In the country we should build our villages near stagnant pools, and particularly encourage settlements in all marshy and unwholesome situations," and so forth and so on.[3]

As a result of this cruel policy, the strong would defeat the weak in the struggle for sur-

Thomas Malthus, who influenced Darwin and proposed that war and scarcity balanced the rapid rise in world population.

vival, and in this way the rapidly increasing population would be balanced. In 19ᵗʰ century England this "crush the poor" programme was actually implemented. An industrial system was founded where children of eight or nine were made to work 16 hours a day in the coal mines and where thousands died from the bad conditions. The theoretical "struggle for survival" which Malthus's theory found necessary, condemned millions of poor people in England to a life full of suffering.

Darwin, influenced by Malthus, applied this view to the whole of nature, and proposed that this war, which actually existed, would be won by the strongest and the fittest. This claim of Darwin's included all plants, animals, and human beings. He also stressed that the struggle for survival in question was a permanent and unchanging law of nature. By denying creation he was inviting people to abandon their religious beliefs and in this way aiming at all ethical principles that might be an obstacle to the ruthlessness of this "struggle for survival."

For this reason Darwin's theory found the support of the Establishment at its back, right from the moment it came to be heard, first in England and later in the entire West. The imperialists, capitalists and other materialists who greeted this theory, which provided a scientific justification for the political and social system they had founded, did not delay in taking it up. Within a short time the theory of evolution was brought to be the sole criterion in every sphere of interest to human societies, from sociology to history, from psychology to politics. In every sphere the basic idea was the slogan of the "fight for survival" and "the survival of the fittest," and political parties, nations, administrations, commercial firms, and individuals began to live in the warmth of these slogans. Because the ruling ideologies in society had identified with Darwinism, Darwinist propaganda began to be carried out in every field, from education to art, from politics to history. It was attempted to establish links between every subject and Darwinism and to shed light on them from a Darwinist viewpoint. As a result of this, even if people did not know Darwinism, models of society living the lives predicted by Darwinism began to be formed.

Darwin himself recommended that his views based on evolution be applied to ethical understanding and social sciences. Darwin said the following to H. Thiel in a letter in 1869:

> **You will readily believe how much interested I am in observing that you apply to moral and social questions analogous views to those which I have used in regard to the modification of species.** It did not occur to me formerly that my views could be extended to such widely different, and most important, subjects.[4]

With the struggle in nature also being accepted as being in human nature, conflicts in the name of racism, Fascism, Communism, and imperialism, and the efforts of strong peoples to crush peoples they perceived as weaker were by now clothed in a scien-

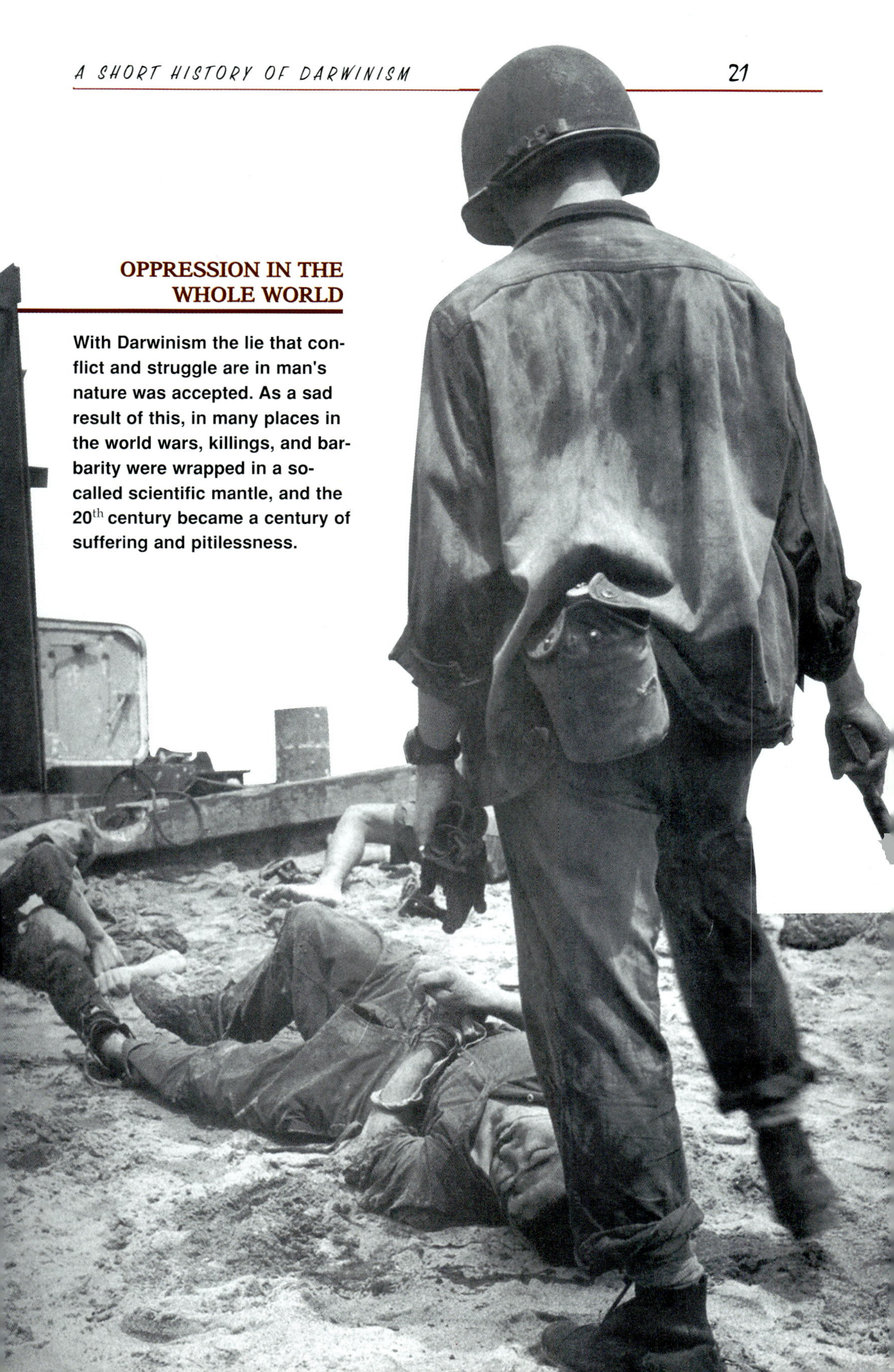

OPPRESSION IN THE WHOLE WORLD

With Darwinism the lie that conflict and struggle are in man's nature was accepted. As a sad result of this, in many places in the world wars, killings, and barbarity were wrapped in a so-called scientific mantle, and the 20th century became a century of suffering and pitilessness.

THE PAINFUL BALANCE SHEET

According to Social Darwinism, the weak, poor, sick, and backward must be eliminated, and done away with without mercy. These people believe that this is necessary for the evolution of mankind. One of the reasons why in the 20th century no answer came to millions of peoples' cries for help, from Bosnia to Ethiopia, was this ideology which was ruthlessly imposed on societies.

tific façade. It was now impossible to reproach or obstruct those who carried out barbarous massacres, treated human beings like animals, turned peoples against each other, who despised others on account of their race, who closed down small businesses in the name of competition, and who refused to extend the hand of help to the poor. Because they were doing this in accordance with a "scientific" natural law.

This new scientific account came to be known as **"Social Darwinism."**

One of the foremost evolutionist scientists of our own time, the American palaeontologist Stephen Jay Gould accepts the truth by writing that following the publication of *The Origin of Species* in 1859, "subsequent arguments for slavery, colonialism, racial differences, class struggles, and sex roles would go forth primarily under the banner of science."[5]

One point requires careful attention here. All periods of human history have seen wars, atrocities, ruthlessness, racism, and conflict. But there was at all times a divine religion teaching people that what they were doing was wrong and calling them to peace, justice, and calm. Because human beings knew this divine religion, they at least had a measure of understanding that what they were doing was wrong when they engaged in violence. But from the 19th century, Darwinism showed that the struggle for profit and injustice had an element of scientific justification to them, and said that all of these were part of human nature, that man carried savage and aggressive tendencies left over from his ancestors, and that in the same way that as the strongest and most aggressive animal survived, the same laws applied to human beings. Under the influence of this thinking, wars, suffering, and massacres began to affect a very large part of the world. Darwinism supported and encouraged all those movements which brought pain, blood, and oppression to the world, showed them to be reasonable and justified, and backed all their practical applications. As a result of this so-called scientific backing all these dangerous ideologies grew increasingly stronger, and stamped the name "the age of suffering" on the 20th century.

In his book *Darwin, Marx, Wagner* professor of history Jacques

The author of *"Darwin, Marx, Wagner,"* professor of history Jacques Barzun.

Barzun evaluates the scientific, sociological, and cultural causes of the terrible moral breakdown of the modern world. These comments from Barzun's book are striking from the point of view of Darwinism's influence on the world:

… in every European country between 1870 and 1914 there was a war party demanding armaments, an individualist party demanding ruthless competition, an imperialist party demanding a free hand over backward peoples, a socialist party demanding the conquest of power, and a racialist party demanding internal purges against aliens–all of them, when appeals to greed and glory failed, or even before, invoked Spencer and Darwin, which was to say, science incarnate… Race was biological, it was sociological, it was Darwinian.[6]

In the 19th century, when Darwin put forward his claim that living things had not been created, that they had emerged by coincidence, and that the human being had a common ancestor with animals and had emerged as the most highly developed organism as the result of coincidence, perhaps most people could not imagine what the results of this claim would be. But in the 20th century the end result of the claim was lived out in terrible experiences. Those who saw human beings as a developed animal, did not hesitate to rise by treading on the weak, to find a way of disposing of the sick and weak, and to carry out massacres to get rid of races which they saw as different and inferior. Because their theory with a mask of science told them that this was a "law of nature."

The disasters Darwinism brought to the world began in this way, and gathering speed, spread over the whole world. Whereas in the 19th century, until materialism and atheism grew stronger through the support they received from Darwinism, the great majority of people believed that God created all living things and that human beings, unlike other living creatures, possessed a soul created by God. From whatever race or people, human beings were each seen as a servant created by God. Lack of religion, however, brought about and strengthened by Darwinism, gave rise to social groups with a competitive and ruthless world view, attaching no importance to morals, seeing human beings as highly developed animals. People who denied that they had any responsibility to God brought about a culture where every type of selfishness was justified. From this culture were born many "isms," and each of these became a calamity, in the real sense of the world, for mankind.

In the following pages we will examine the ideologies in question to which Darwinism lent justification, the close relationships between these ideologies and Darwinism, and what this co-operation has cost the world.

PART 2

DARWIN'S RACISM AND COLONIALISM

Darwin's close friend Professor Adam Sedgwick was one of the people who saw what dangers the theory of evolution would give rise to in the future. He remarked, after reading and digesting *The Origin of Species*, that **"if this book were to find general public acceptance, it would bring with it a brutalisation of the human race such as it had never seen before."**[7] And truly, time showed that Sedgwick was right to have doubts. The 20th century has gone down in history as a dark age when people underwent massacres simply because of their race or ethnic origins.

Of course, there were discrimination and eradication based on it in human history long before Darwin. **But Darwinism lent this discrimination a false scientific respectability and a false rightfulness.**

Professor Adam Sedgwick

"**The Preservation of Favoured Races...**"

Most Darwinists in our day claim that Darwin was never a racist but that racists comment on Darwin's ideas in a biased manner for the purpose of supporting their own views. They claim that the expression *"By the Preservation of Favoured Races"* in the subtitle to *The Origin of Species* is used only for animals. However, what those who make this claim ignore is what Darwin says about human races in his book.

According to the views put forward by Darwin in this book, human races represent different stages of evolution, and some races have evolved and progressed more than others. Some of them, in fact, were pretty much at the same level as monkeys.

Darwin claimed that the "fight for survival" also applied between human races. "Favoured races" emerged victorious from this struggle. According to Darwin the favoured race were the European whites. As for Asian and African races, they had fallen behind in the fight for survival. Darwin went even further: these races would soon completely lose the world-wide fight for survival and disappear, he claimed.

> At some future period, not very distant as measured by centuries, the civilised races of man will almost certainly exterminate, and replace, the savage races throughout the world. At the same time the anthropomorphous apes ... will no doubt be exterminated. The break between man and his nearest allies will then be wider, for it will intervene between man in a more civilised state, as we may hope, even than the Caucasian, and some ape **as low as a baboon, instead of as now between the negro or Australian and the gorilla.**[8]

Again in another part of *The Origin of Species*, Darwin claimed that it was necessary for the inferior races to disappear and that there was no need for developed peoples to try to protect them and keep them alive. He compared this situation to people who raised breeding animals:

> **With savages, the weak in body or mind are soon eliminated;** and those that survive commonly exhibit a vigorous state of health. We civilised men, on the other hand, do our utmost to check the process of elimination; we build asylums for the imbecile, the maimed, and the sick; we institute poor-laws; and our medical men exert their utmost skill to save the life of every one to the last moment. There is reason to believe that vaccination has preserved thousands, who from a weak constitution would formerly have succumbed to small-pox. Thus the weak members of civilised societies propagate their kind. No one who has attended to the breeding of domestic animals will doubt that this must be highly injurious to the race of man.[9]

As we have seen, in his book *The Origin of Species* Darwin saw the natives of Australia and Negroes as being at the same level as gorillas and claimed that these races would disappear. As for the other races which he saw as "inferior," he maintained that it was essential to prevent them multiplying and so for these races to be brought to extinction. So the traces of racism and discrimination which we still come across in our time were approved and lent justification by Darwin in this way.

As for the task befalling the "civilised person," according to Darwin's racist idea, it was to speed this evolutionary period up a little, as we shall see in the details which follow. In this situation there was no objection, from the "scientific" point of view, to these races, which were going to disappear anyway, being done away with now.

Darwin's racist side showed its effect in much of his writing and observations. For example, he openly set out his racist prejudices while describing the natives of Tierra del Fuego whom he saw on a long voyage he set out on in 1871. He described the natives as living creatures "wholly nude, submerged in dyes, eating what they find just like wild animals, uncontrolled, cruel to everybody out of their tribe, taking pleasure in torturing their enemies, offering bloddy sacrifices, killing their children, ill-treating their wives, full of awkward superstitions". Whereas the researcher W. P. Snow, who had travelled the same region ten years before, presents a very different picture. According to Snow, the Tierra del Fuegians were "fine powerful looking fellows; they were very fond of their children; some of their artefacts were ingenious; they recognised some sort of rights over property; and they accepted the authority of several of the oldest women."[10]

As has been seen from these examples Darwin was a

The journeys Darwin embarked on revealed his racist side. For example, Darwin considered the term "wild animals" suitable for tribes whose culture and abilities other researchers had discussed.

complete racist. As a matter of fact, in the words of the author of the book *What Darwin Really Said*, Benjamin Farrington, Darwin made many comments regarding **"the greater differences between men of distinct races"** in his book *The Descent of Man*.[11]

Furthermore, Darwin's theory's denying the existence of God had been the cause of peoples' not seeing that man was something created by God and that all men were created equal. And this was one of the factors behind the rise of racism and the acceleration of its acceptance in the world. The American scientist James Ferguson announces the strict link between the denial of creation and the rise of racism in this way:

> The new anthropology soon became a theoretical background between two opposed schools of thought on the origin of humans. The older and more established of these was 'monogenism,' the belief that all humankind, irrespective of colour and other characteristics, was directly descended from Adam and from the single and original act of God's creation. Monogenism was promulgated by the Church and universally accepted until the 18th century, when **opposition to theological authority began to fuel the rival theory of 'polygenism,' (theory of evolution)** which held that different racial communities had different origins.[12]

The Indian anthropologist Lalita Vidyarthi explains how Darwin's theory of evolution led racism to be accepted by social sciences:

> **His (Darwin's) theory of the survival of the fittest** was warmly welcomed by the social scientists of the day, and they believed mankind had achieved various levels of evolution culminating in the white man's civilization. **By the second half of the nineteenth century racism was accepted as fact by the vast majority of Western scientists.**[13]

As for the Darwinists who came after Darwin, they put up a great struggle to prove his racist views. In the name of doing so they had no scruples about making many scientific inconsistencies and falsehoods. They thought that when they had proved these, they would have scientifically proven their own superiority and "rights" to oppress, colonise, and if needs be exterminate other races.

In the third chapter of his book *The Mismeasure of Man*, Stephen Jay

Gould pointed out that some anthropologists were not above falsifying their data to prove the "superiority" of the white race. According to Gould, the method they used most was falsifying the brain size of the fossilised skulls they found. Gould mentions in his book that, assuming brain size had something to do with intelligence, many anthropologists intentionally exaggerated the size of Caucasian skulls and underestimated the size of skulls from Blacks and Indians.[14]

In his book *Ever Since Darwin*, Gould explains the unbelievable claims the Darwinists undertook to demonstrate that some races were inferior.

> Haeckel and his colleagues also invoked recapitulation to affirm the racial superiority of northern European whites. They scoured the evidence of human anatomy and behaviour, using everything they could find from brains to belly buttons. Herbert Spencer wrote that "the intellectual traits of the uncivilized.. are traits recurring in the children of the civilized." Carl Vogt said it more strongly in 1864: "The grown up Negro partakes, as regards his intellectual faculties, of the nature of the child... Some tribes have founded states, possessing a peculiar organization, but, as to the rest, we may boldly assert that the whole race has, neither in the past nor in the present, performed anything tending to the progress of humanity or worthy of preservation."[15]

And the French medical anatomist Etienne Serres really did argue that black males are primitive because their belly buttons were in a lower level.

Darwin's contemporary, the evolutionist Havelock Ellis, supported the distinction between superior and inferior races with an alleged "scientific" explanation, saying:

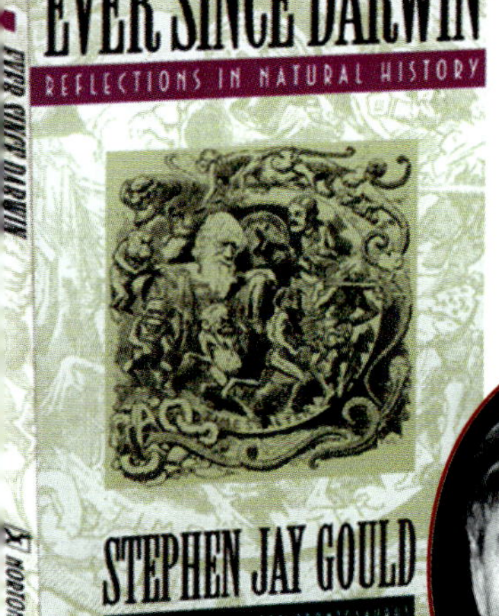

Stephen Jay Gould and his book which revealed Darwin's racist side.

The child of many African races is scarcely if at all less intelligent than the European child, but while the African as he grows up becomes stupid and obtuse, and his whole social life falls into a state of hidebound routine, the European retains much of his childlike vivacity.[16]

The French Darwinist anthropologist Vacher de Lapouge suggested, in his work titled *Race et Milin Social Essais d'Anthroposociologie* (Paris 1909) that non-white classes were the descendants of savages who had not learnt to be civilised, or else the degenerate representatives of mixed-blood classes. He produced results by measuring the skulls from Paris' upper and lower classes in graveyards. According to his results, depending on their skulls some people were inclined to be rich, self-confident, and free, and others conservative, content with little, and possessing all the qualities of a good servant, classes were the products of social selection, society's upper classes went together with superior races, the degree of wealth was in proportion to the skull index. Lapouge later made a prophesy, "It is my view that in years to come people will kill each other because their heads are round or pointed," he said[17], and this prophesy came true, as we shall see in detail in later pages of this book, and the 20th century saw massacres carried out for reasons of racism…!

And it was not only anthropologists: entomologists (those who study insects) also jumped on the racist bandwagon that Darwinism had set in motion with unbelievable claims. For example, in the year 1861, one English entomologist arrived at the conclusion, after collecting lice that lived on peoples' bodies in different parts of the world, that the lice of one race could not live on the bodies of another, which when looked at from the scientific level of today, is just plain ridiculous.[18] When even people with the status of scientists made such announcements, it was not surprising that some dogmatic racists should use such illogical, unintelligent, and completely meaningless slogans as "even Negroes' lice are Negro."

In short, the racist side to Darwin's theory found very fertile ground in the second half of the 19th century. Because at that time the European "white man" was still waiting for such a theory to justify his own crimes.

British Colonialism and Darwinism

The country which profited most from Darwin's racist views was Darwin's own land, Britain. In the years when Darwin put forward his theory, Great Britain was in the position of having founded the world's number one colonialist empire. All the natural resources of an area stretching from India to Latin America were exploited by the British Empire. The "white man" was plundering the world for his own interests.

But, of course, starting with Great Britain, no colonialist country wanted to be seen as a "plunderer" and to go down in history as such. For this reason, they were looking for an explanation to show that they were right in what they were doing. Such an explanation might be to portray the colonised peoples as "primitive people" or "animal-like living creatures." In this way, for those who were massacred and subjected to inhuman treatment to be able to be seen not as human beings, but as half-human half-animal creatures, and their mistreatment would not be regarded as a crime.

Actually, this search was not new: the first spread of colonialism in the world went back to the 15th and 16th centuries. Claims to the effect that some races had semi-animal characteristics were first put forward by Christopher Columbus on his American journey. According to these claims, Native Americans were not human beings, but a species of developed animal. For this reason they could be put to the service of the Spanish colonialists.

No matter how much Columbus is portrayed in films about the discovery of America as having a warm and humane attitude to the natives, the fact is that Columbus did not regard the native people as human.[19]

Christopher Columbus was the person who first set in motion a great massacre. Columbus established Spanish colonies in the places he discovered, made slaves of the natives and was responsible for the starting of the slave trade. The Spanish "conquistadors" saw the policy of oppression and exploitation that Columbus implemented, and continued it: the massacres carried out reached unbelievable dimensions. For example, the population of one island, 200,000 when Columbus first came to it, was only 50,000 20 years later, and by 1540 only a thousand people remained. When the most famous of the Spanish conquistadors, Cortes, first set foot in Mexico in February 1519, the total native population was 25 million, but in 1605 this had fallen to 1 million. On the island of Hispaniola, the population, which was 7-8 million in 1492, fell to 4 million in 1496, and to just 125 people in 1570. According to historians' figures, in less than a century after Columbus first set foot on the continent **95 million were massacred by the colonialists**. When Columbus discovered America 30 million natives were living on the continent. As a result of the massacres between then and now they have come to the position of being a lost race of less than 2 million.

The reason for these massacres reaching such pitiless proportions was the indigenous peoples' not being seen as human beings, as being looked on as animals.

But these claims of the colonialists did not win many supporters. In Europe at that time, the truth that all people were created equal by God

THE MASSACRE OF THE NATIVE AMERICANS

With Christopher Columbus' discovery of America there began a dreadful massacre of the Native Americans.

and that they all descended from one ancestor–Adam–was so widely accepted that the Catholic Church in particular took a clear position against such plundering invasions. One of the best known examples of this is the reply by the bishop of Chiapas, Bartolome de las Casas, who set foot in the New World together with Columbus, who said that the natives were "each a real human being," in reply to the colonists' claim that the natives were "a species of animal." Pope Paul III cursed the savage treatment of the natives in a papal bull in 1537, and declared that the natives were real human beings with the capacity for faith.[20]

But in the 19th century the situation changed. Together with the spread of materialist philosophy and societies' growing distant from religion, the truth that human beings were created by God began to be denied. This, as was touched on in the preceding pages, was at the same time the rise of racism.

With the rise of Darwinist-materialist philosophy in the 19th century, racism grew stronger, and this created a great support for Europe's imperialist system.

James Joll, who spent long years as professor of history at such universities as Oxford, Stanford and Harvard, in his source book *Europe Since 1870*, which is still used as a text book in universities, describes the ideological relationship between Darwinism, imperialism, and racism.

> The most profound groups of ideas inspiring the concept of imperialism were those which can be roughly classified as 'social Darwinism', and which saw the relations between states as a perpetual struggle for survival in which some races were regarded as 'superior' to others in an evolutionary process in which the strongest had constantly to assert themselves.

> Charles Darwin, the English naturalist whose books *On the Origin of Species*, published in 1859, and *The Descent of Man*, which followed in 1871,

Queen Victoria and the principal actor in the above massacres, the Spaniard Cortes.

launched controversies which affected many branches of European thought... The ideas of Darwin, and of some of his contemporaries such as the English philosopher Herbert Spencer, ...were rapidly applied to questions far removed from the immediate scientific ones... The element of Darwinism which appeared most applicable to the development of society was the belief that the excess of population over the means of support necessitated a constant struggle for survival in which it was the strongest or the 'fittest' who won. From this it was easy for some social thinkers to give a moral content to the notion of the fittest, so that the species or races which did survive were those morally entitled to do so.

The doctrine of natural selection could, therefore, very easily become associated with another train of thought developed by the French writer, Count Joseph-Arthur Gobineau, who published an *Essay on the Inequality of Human Races* in 1853. Gobineau insisted that the most important factor in development was race; and that those races which remained superior were those which kept their racial purity intact. Of these, according to Gobineau, it was the Aryan race which had survived best... It was.. Houston Stewart Chamberlain who contributed to carrying some of these ideas a stage further... Hitler himself admired the author (Chamberlain) sufficiently to visit him on his deathbed in 1927.[21]

As has been shown, there is an ideological chain linking Darwin to racist thinkers and imperialists, and stretching from there as far as Hitler. Darwinism is the ideological basis of both imperialism, which drowned the world in blood in the 19th century, and Nazism, which did the same thing in the 20th.

Victorian Great Britain also found its so-called "scientific basis" in Darwinism. Great Britain made great profits out of colonialism, and saw no reason not to visit disasters upon the heads of those living under that colonialism for its own advantage. One example of British imperialism's dirty politics was the "Opium Wars" against China. Great Britain began to smuggle the opium it grew in India into China from the first quarter of the 19th century. This opium smuggling was speeded up as time passed to make good the deficit in its foreign trade. The flow of the drug into the country also had the effect of weakening the Chinese state's authority over its own territory. The collapse in society soon reached serious dimensions. The prohibition of opium, which the Chinese government had to implement after a long period of doubt, led to the first Opium War (1838-1842). There is no doubt that this war dragged the country to bankruptcy. China was forced to bow its head because of the inadequacy of its army in every confrontation with the foreign forces and to accept their ever-growing demands. The Westerners slowly formed settlement centres inside Chinese territory from the year 1842. They took large port quarters (concessions) from out of the hands of the Chinese, rented their fields, and obliged the country to open up to the outside world in a way that would

PILTDOWN MAN FORGERY

One of the most interesting indications of the inspiration the theory of evolution offered to British imperialism, was the Piltdown man scandal.

In 1912, a strange skull was found in Piltdown, England. Charles Dawson, the scientist who found the skull together with his team, declared that it belonged to a creature which was half ape-half human. Arthur Keith, the renowned evolutionist anatomist examined the fossil and confirmed the results.

However, Dawson and Keith emphasised an important point. The brain of the fossil was as big as that of modern man. The jawbone, however, had ape-like features.

Suddenly the brain of Piltdown man became a matter of pride for the British. Since this skull was found in England, it had to be the ancestor of the British. According to the British people, the greater volume of the brain indicated that British had evolved before other races, and were thus superior to other races.

That is why the discovery of Piltdown man aroused great excitement in England. Newspapers ran headlines and crowds joyously celebrated the discovery. The British government, on the other hand, granted a knighthood to Arthur Keith for his famous discovery.

The famous evolutionist palaeontologist, Don Johanson, describes the relationship between the Piltdown fossil and English imperialism:

> The Piltdown discovery was very eurocentric. Not only did the brain have pre-eminence, but the English had pre-eminence, too.*

The inspiration the English derived from Piltdown man lasted only until 1953, when Kenneth Oakley, a scientist who re-examined the fossil in detail, revealed it to be the greatest forgery of the 20th century. The fossil had been produced by affixing an orang-utan jaw to a human skull.

*Don Johanson, *In Search of Human Origins*, 1994 WGBH Educational Foundation bring the most benefit to themselves. As a result of all of this, the poverty in the country, the weakness of the government, and the slow loss of Chinese territory led to many rebellions.

The experiences in China were only one of the results of British policy. Throughout the 19th century the oppression and painful dimensions of British imperialism were experienced in such regions as South Africa, India, and Australia.

The job of justifying this oppressive system of Britain's and attempting to show it was in the right, fell to various British sociologists and scientists. And Charles Darwin was the most important and effective of these. It was Darwin who claimed that throughout evolution there had been "superior races," that these were the "white race," and showed that the whites' oppression of the others was a "natural law."

Because of the justification which Darwin provided for colonialist racism, the famous scientist, Kenneth J. Hsü, the head of the Geography department of the Swiss Federal Institute of Technology and himself of Chinese descent, describes Darwin as "a gentleman scientist of the Victorian Era, and an establishment member of a society that sent gunboats to forcibly import opium into China, **all in the name of competition (in free trade) and survival of the fittest.**"[22]

Darwin's Enmity Towards the Turks

The most important target British colonialism set itself towards the end of the 19th century was the Ottoman Empire.

At that period the Ottoman state ruled a huge area from Yemen to Bosnia-Herzegovina. But by now it was finding it hard to control this area which it had managed in peace, calm, and stability. Christian minorities were beginning to rise up in the name of independence, and such great military powers as Russia were beginning to threaten the Ottomans.

In the last quarter of the century Britain and France joined the powers which were threatening the Ottomans. Britain particularly set its eyes on the Ottomans' southern provinces. The Berlin Agreement, signed in 1878, is an expression of the European colonialists' decision to divide up the Ottoman territories. Five years later, in 1882, Britain occupied Egypt, which was an Ottoman territory. British colonialism set about its plans to later take over the Ottoman territories in the Middle East.

As always, Britain based these colonialist policies on racism. The British government deliberately tried to portray the Turkish nation, the basic element of the Ottomans, and particularly the Ottoman state, as a so-called "backward" people.

British Prime Minister William Ewart Gladstone openly said that the Turks are examples of mankind's non-humans, and for the sake of their civilisation, they must be pushed back to the Asian steppes and eliminated from Anatolia.[23]

These, and words like them, were for decades used by the British government as a propaganda tool directed against the Ottomans. Britain

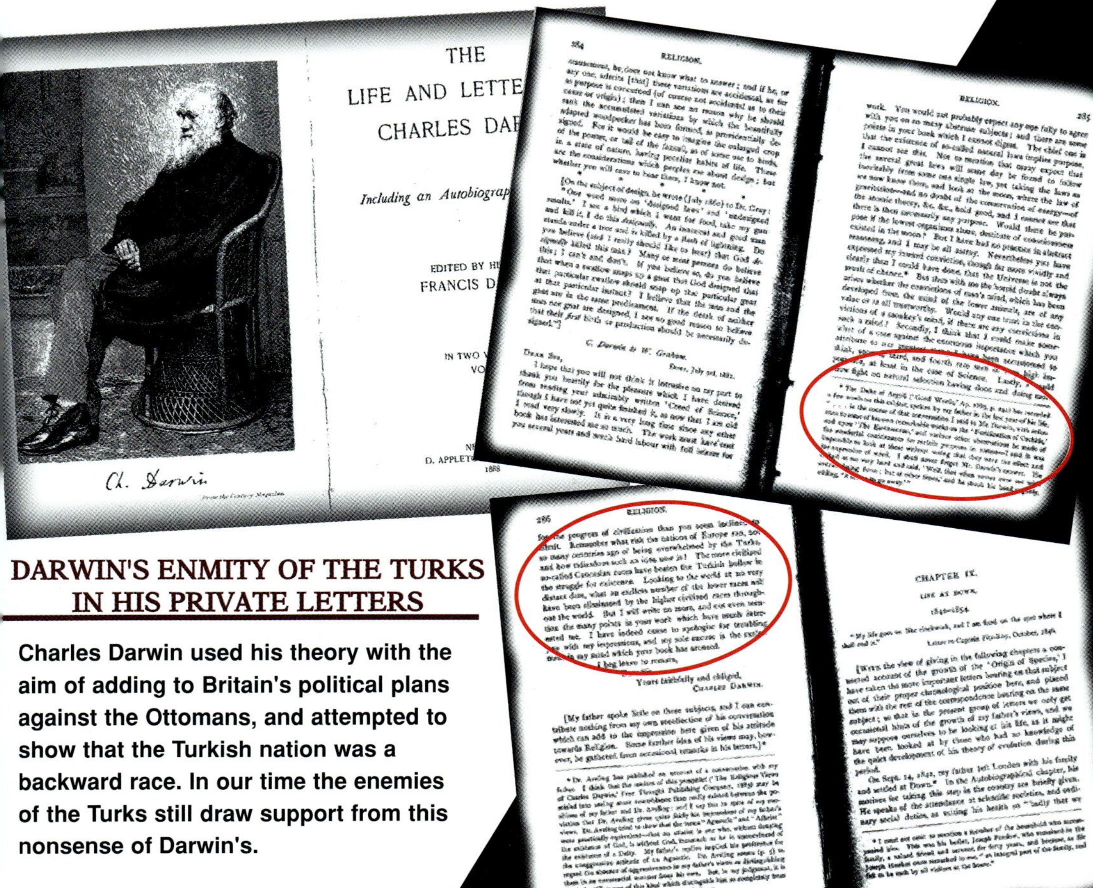

DARWIN'S ENMITY OF THE TURKS IN HIS PRIVATE LETTERS

Charles Darwin used his theory with the aim of adding to Britain's political plans against the Ottomans, and attempted to show that the Turkish nation was a backward race. In our time the enemies of the Turks still draw support from this nonsense of Darwin's.

tried to portray the Turkish nation as a backward nation that had to bow its head to more advanced European races.

The so-called "scientific basis" for this propaganda was Charles Darwin!

Darwin's comments regarding the Turkish nation appeared in the book *The Life and Letters of Charles Darwin*, published in 1888. Darwin proposed that by eliminating the "backward races" natural selection would play a role in the development of civilisation, and later said these exact words about the Turkish nation:

> I could show fight on natural selection having done and doing more for the progress of civilization than you seem inclined to admit. Remember what risk the nations of Europe ran, not so many centuries ago of being overwhelmed by the Turks, and how ridiculous such an idea now is! The more civilized so-called Caucasian races have beaten the Turkish hollow in the struggle for existence. Looking to the world at no very distant date, what an endless number of the lower races will have been eliminated by the higher civilized races throughout the world.[24]

This nonsense of Darwin's was a written propaganda tool to give support to Britain's policy of destroying the Ottoman Empire. And in fact this propaganda tool was an effective one. Darwin's words to the effect that "The Turkish nation will soon disappear, this is a law of evolution" gave a so-called scientific support to Britain's propaganda directed at creating enmity towards the Turks.

Britain's desire to bring about Darwin's prophecy basically came to life in the First World War. This giant war, which began in 1914, was born of conflicts of interest between Germany and Austria-Hungary on the one side, and the allies Britain, France, and Russia on the other. But one of the

THE GALLIPOLI CAMPAIGN

In the Gallipoli campaign the Turkish Army heroically fought against the enemy forces, with the British at their head, and lost 250,000 men.

most important calculations within this war was the aim of destroying and dividing up the Ottoman Empire.

Britain attacked the Ottoman Empire from two separate directions. The first was the Canal, Palestine, and Iraq fronts, opened with the intention of taking the Ottoman territories in the Middle East. The second was the Gallipoli front, scene of one of the bloodiest battles of the First World War. The Turkish Army at Çanakkale fought heroically and lost 250,000 men to resist the enemy forces mustered by the British. As for the British, they sent more Indian troops and Anzac units recruited from such colonies as Australia and New Zealand to fight the Turks, whom they saw as a "backward race," than their own soldiers.

The echoes of Darwin's hostility to the Turks continued to ring after the First World War. The European Neo-Nazi groups who treacherously attack the Turks in Europe still draw their inspiration from Darwin's stupid nonsense about the Turkish nation. Darwin's words about the Turks are still to be found on the Internet pages of these racist enemies of the Turks. (See the chapter on The Bloody Alliance Between Darwin and Hitler.)

Racism and Social Darwinism in America

Social Darwinism provided support for racists and imperialists in other countries too, not just Britain. For this reason it spread quickly through the whole world. At the head of those subscribing to the theory came U.S. President Theodore Roosevelt. Roosevelt was the foremost proponent and implementer of the programme of ethnic cleansing applied against the Native Americans under the name of "forced relocation." In the book *The Winning of the West*, he founded the ideology of massacre, maintaining that a racial war to the finish with the Indians was inevitable.[25] His greatest prop was Darwinism, which gave him the chance to define the natives as a backward species.

As Roosevelt had foreseen, none of the treaties with the Native Americans were respected, and this too was provided a false justification under the "backward race" theory. In 1871, Congress disregarded all the treaties made with the Native Americans and decided to exile them to dead lands where they could await death. If the other side were not perceived as human beings then how could the treaties made with them have any validity?

Roosevelt also proposed that the above mentioned racial war represented the culminating achievement of the spread of the English speaking peoples (Anglo-Saxons) over the world.[26]

One of the foremost proponents of Anglo-Saxon racism, the American evolutionist and Protestant clergyman Josiah Strong, employed the same logic. He once wrote these words:

> Then will the world enter upon a new stage of its history - the final competition of races for which the Anglo-Saxon is being schooled. If I do not read amiss, this powerful race will move down upon Mexico, down upon Central and South America, out upon the islands of the sea, over upon Africa and beyond. And can anyone doubt that **the result of this competition will be "survival of the fittest"**?[27]

The foremost of the racists who used Social Darwinism to justify themselves were the enemies of the blacks. Their racist theories, which divided the races into levels and defined the white race as the most superior and the black race as the most primitive, enthusiastically embraced the concept of evolution.[28]

The most prominent of the evolutionary racist theoreticians, Henry Fairfield Osborn, wrote in an article headed *The Evolution of Human Races* that "The standard of intelligence of the average adult Negro is similar to that of the eleven-year-old-youth of the species Homo Sapiens."[29]

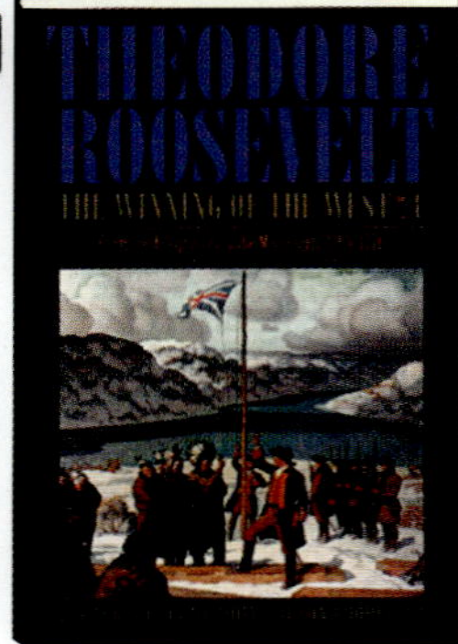

In his book *The Winning of the West*, US President Theodore T. Roosevelt established the ideology of massacre, and later implemented it.

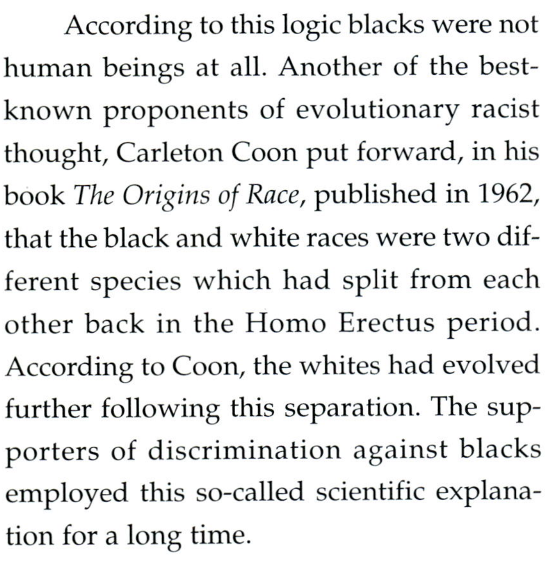

According to this logic blacks were not human beings at all. Another of the best-known proponents of evolutionary racist thought, Carleton Coon put forward, in his book *The Origins of Race*, published in 1962, that the black and white races were two different species which had split from each other back in the Homo Erectus period. According to Coon, the whites had evolved further following this separation. The supporters of discrimination against blacks employed this so-called scientific explanation for a long time.

The existence of a scientific theory which supported it rapidly increased racism in America. W. E. Dubois, known for being against racial discrimination, stated that "the problem of the twentieth century is the problem of the colour line". According to him, that the problem of racism should have emerged in such a widespread manner in a country which wants to become the world's greatest democracy, and which from some points of view has accomplished this, is not the least important of paradoxes. The abolition of slavery has not sufficed

In late 19th and early 20th century America, whites treated blacks quite ruthlessly. Laws and their applications clearly revealed that blacks were not regarded as human beings. While the whites lived in great wealth, blacks received inhuman treatment.

for the establishment of brotherhood between black and white people. He thought that official discrimination, set up in a short time, has in our day turned into an ipso facto and legal situation, a way out of which is still being sought.[30]

The emergence of the first racial discrimination laws, known as the "Jim Crow Laws," (Jim Crow was one of the derogatory names for blacks used by the whites) also happened at this time. Blacks

THE OPPRESSION OF THE BLACKS

The Ku Klux Klan was the group that carried out the most ruthless attacks against blacks. The chain in the picture to the side was used to chain black slaves to one another.

were definitely not treated like human beings, and were despised and treated with contempt everywhere: furthermore this was not the attitude of a few racist individuals but that determined by the American state by its own laws. Immediately after the first law approving racial segregation on railways and trams was passed in Tennessee in 1875, all the Southern states implemented segregation on their railways. "Whites Only" and "Blacks" signs were hung up everywhere. Actually, all of these just meant the granting of official status to a situation which already existed. Marriage between different races was forbidden. Under the law, segregation was compulsory in hospitals, prisons, and graveyards. In practice, this included hotels, theatres, libraries, and even lifts and churches. The field where segregation was most sharply felt was in schools. This was the practice which had the heaviest effects on the blacks and was the greatest obstacle in the face of their cultural development.

The practice of racial segregation was accompanied by a wave of violence. There was a swift rise in the number of black lynchings. Between 1890 and 1901 some 1,300 blacks were lynched. As a result of these implementations blacks rose up in several states.

Racist thought and theories accompanied this period. Shortly after, American biological racism would express itself in the results arrived at by R. B. Bean's method of skull measurement, and under the pretence of protecting the people of the new continent from a wave of uncontrolled migration, a particular kind of American racism arose. Madison Grant, author of the book *The Passing of the Great Race* (1916) wrote that the mixing of the two races will open the way to the emergence of a more primitive race than the inferior species, and he wanted inter-racial marriages to be banned.[31]

He also wanted inter-racial marriages to be banned.

Racism existed in America before Darwin, as it did in the whole world. But as we have seen, Darwinism gave racist views and policies apparent support in the second half of the 19th century. For example, as we have seen in this chapter, when racists put forward their views they used the claims of Darwinism as slogans. Ideas which before Darwin had been regarded as cruel, now began to be accepted as natural law.

Darwinist Racists' Inhuman Policies

The Extermination of the Aborigines

The natives of Australia are known as aborigines. These people who had lived on the continent for thousands of years suffered one of the biggest exterminations in history with the spreading of European settlers over the country. The ideological basis of this extermination was Darwinism. Darwinist ideologues' views of the aborigines formed the theory of the savagery these people suffered.

In 1870 Max Muller, an evolutionist anthropologist from the *London Anthropological Review*, had divided human races into seven categories. Aborigines appeared at the bottom, and the Aryan race, that of the white Europeans, at the top. H. K. Rusden, a famous Social Darwinist, had this to say about the aborigines in 1876:

The survival of the fittest means that might is right. And we thus invoke and remorselessly fulfil the inexorable law of

THE MASSACRE OF THE ABORIGINES

The natives of Australia, the aborigines, were seen as an undeveloped human species by the evolutionists and were massacred.

natural selection when exterminating the inferior Australian and Maori races... and we appropriate their patrimony coolly.[32]

And in 1890 the Vice-President of the Royal Society of Tasmania, James Barnard, wrote: "the process of extermination is an axiom of the law of evolution and survival of the fittest." There was therefore, he concluded, no reason to suppose that "there had been any culpable neglect" in the murder and dispossession of the Aboriginal Australian.[33]

As a result of these racist, ruthless, and savage views nourished by Darwin, a terrible massacre was begun with the aim of exterminating the aborigines. Aboriginal heads were nailed over station doors. Poisoned bread was given to Aboriginal families. In many parts of Australia, aborigine settlement areas disappeared in a savage manner within 50 years.[34]

The policies aimed at aborigines did not end with massacres. Many members of the race were treated like experimental animals. The Smithsonian Institute in Washington D.C. held the remains of 15,000 people of various races. 10,000 Australian aborigines were sent by ship to the British Museum with the aim of seeing whether or not they were the "missing link" in the transition from animals to human beings.

Museums were not just interested in bones, at the same time they kept brains belonging to aborigines and sold them at good prices. There is also proof that Australian aborigines were killed to be used as specimens. The facts below bear witness to this ruthlessness:

A death-bed memoir from Korah Wills, who became mayor of Bowen, Queensland in 1866, graphically describes how he killed and dismembered a local tribesman in 1865 to provide a scientific specimen.

Edward Ramsay, curator of the Australian Museum in Sydney for 20 years from 1874, was particularly heavily involved. He published a museum booklet which appeared to include Aborigines under the designation of "Australian animals". It also gave instructions not only on how to rob graves, but also on how to plug up bullet wounds in freshly killed "specimens".

A German evolutionist, Amalie Dietrich (nicknamed the 'Angel of Black Death') came to Australia asking station owners for Aborigines to be shot for specimens, particularly skin for stuffing and mounting for her museum employers. Although evicted from at least one property, she shortly returned home with her specimens.

A New South Wales missionary was a horrified witness to the slaughter by mounted police of a group of dozens of Aboriginal men, women and children. Forty-five heads were then boiled down and the 10 best skulls were packed off for overseas.[35]

The extermination of the aborigines continued in the 20th century. Among the methods employed in this extermination was the forcible removal of aborigine children from their families. A news story by Alan Thornhill, which appeared in the 28 April 1997 edition of the *Philadelphia Daily News*, recounted this method used against the aborigines in this way:

ABORIGINE FAMILIES RECOUNT SEIZURES

Associated Press - Aborigines living in Australia's remote northwest deserts used to smear their light-skinned children with charcoal, hoping to keep state welfare agents from taking them away. "The welfare just grabbed you when they found you," one of the stolen children reported, many years later. "Our people would hide us, paint us with charcoal."

"I was taken to Moola Bulla," said one cattler worker who was stolen as a child. "We were about 5 or 6 years old." His tale was one of thousands heard by Australia's Human Rights and Equal Opportunity Commission during its heart-wrenching inquiry into the "stolen generation." From 1910 until the 1970s, some 100,000 aboriginal children were taken from their parents... Light-skinned aboriginal children were seized and handed out to white families for adoption. Dark-skinned children were put in orphanages.[36]

Even now, the pain is so great that most stories were printed anonymously in the commission's final report, "Bringing Them Home." The commission says the actions of the authorities at that time amounted to genocide as the United Nations defines it. The government has refused to follow the inquiry's recommendation that a tribunal be set up to assess compensation payments for the stolen children.

As we have seen, the inhuman treatment, massacres, cruelty, savagery, and exterminations carried out were all justified by Darwinism's theses of "natural selection," "the fight for survival," and "the survival of the fittest."

All these terrible things the Australian natives suffered were just one small part of the catastrophes Darwinism has brought to the world.

Ota Benga

After Darwin claimed in *The Origin of Species* that human beings had developed from a common ancestor they shared with monkeys, the search for fossils to support this scenario began. But some evolutionists believed that "half-monkey half-man" creatures might be found not only in the fossil record, but also living in various parts of the world. At the beginning of the 20th century the searches for the "missing link" were the cause of many acts of savagery. One of these was the story of the pigmy Ota Benga.

Ota Benga was captured in the Congo by an evolutionist researcher called Samuel Verner in 1904. This native, whose name meant "friend" in his own language, was married and the father of two children. But he was chained like an animal, put in a cage, and sent to the U.S.A. There, the evolutionary scientists put him in a cage with various species of monkey at the St. Louis World

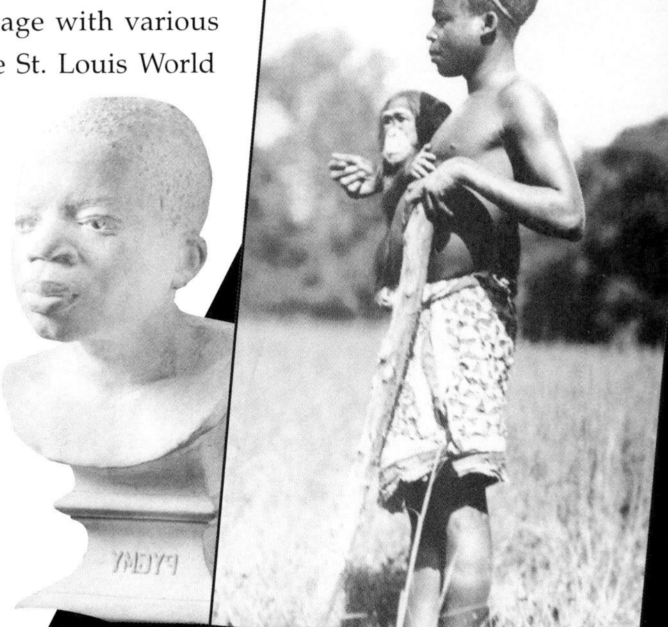

OTA BENGA

Ota Benga was a native of Africa. He was trapped like an animal by evolutionary researchers, put in a cage, and exhibited alongside monkeys in a zoo.

Fair and exhibited him as "the nearest link to man." Two years later they took him to Bronx Zoo in New York and displayed him with a few chimpanzees, a gorilla called Dinah and an orang-utan called Dohung as "man's oldest ancestors." The evolutionist director of the zoo, Dr. William T. Horniday, gave long talks about the pride it gave him to have the "missing link," and visitors treated Ota Benga in his cage just like an animal. An edition of the *New York Times* printed at the time described the visitors' attitudes:

> There were 40,000 visitors to the park on Sunday. Nearly every man woman and child of this crowd made for the monkey house to see the star attraction in the park–the wild man from Africa. They chased him about the grounds all day, howling, jeering, and yelling. Some of them poked him in the ribs, other tripped him up, all laughed at him.[37]

The 17 September 1906 edition of the *New York Journal* said that this was being done to prove evolution, but attacked it as a great injustice and cruelty in these words:

> These men, without thought and intelligence have been exhibiting in a cage of monkeys, a small human dwarf from Africa. **Their idea, probably, was to inculcate some profound lesson in evolution.**
>
> As a matter of fact, the only result achieved has been to hold up to scorn the African race, which deserves at least sympathy and kindness from the whites of this country, after all the brutality it has suffered here...
>
> It is shameful and disgusting that the misfortune, the physical deficiency, of a human being, created by the same Force that puts us all here and endowed with the same feelings and the same soul, should be locked in a cage with monkeys and be made a public mockery.[38]

The *New York Daily Tribune* also gave space to the subject of Ota Benga's being exhibited in the zoo for the purposes of demonstrating evolution. The Darwinist zoo director's defence was completely unscrupulous:

> The exhibition of an African pygmy in the same cage with an orang outang at the New York Zoological Park last week stirred up considerable criticism. Some persons **declared it was an attempt on the part of Director Hornaday to demonstrate a close relationship between Negroes and monkeys.** Dr. Hornaday denied this. "If the little fellow is in a cage," said Dr. Hornaday, "it

is because he is most comfortable there, and because we are at a loss to know what else to do with him. He is in no sense a prisoner, except that no one would say it was wise to allow him to wander around the city without some one having an eye on him."[39]

Ota Benga's being exhibited in the zoo with gorillas like an animal led to unease in various circles. A number of foundations applied to the authorities to have the practice stopped, stating that Ota Benga was a human being and that his being treated in that way was a great cruelty. One of these applications appeared in the *New York Globe* of 12 September 1906 in this way:

Editor of the Globe:

Sir - I lived in the south several years, and consequently am not overfond of negro, but believe him human. I think it a shame that the authorities of this great city should allow such a sight as that witnessed at the Bronx Park - a negro boy, on exhibition in a monkey cage...

This whole pygmy business needs investigation...

A.E.R.

New York, Sept. 12[40]

Another application asking Ota Benga to be treated like a human was as follows:

Man and Monkey Show Disapproved by Clergy

The Rev. Dr. MacArthur Thinks the Exhibition Degrading

"The person responsible for this exhibition degrades himself as much as he does the African" said Dr. MacArthur "Instead of making a beast of this little fellow, he should be put in school for the development of such powers as God gave to him."

Dr. Gilbert said he had already decided that the exhibition was an outrage and that he and other pastors would join with Dr. MacArthur in seeing to it that the Bushman was released from the monkey cage and put elsewhere.[41]

The end result of all this inhuman treatment was Ota Benga's suicide. But here the problem was greater than that of one human being losing his life. This event was a clear example of the cruelty and savagery that Darwinist racism could mean in practice.

THE ESKIMOS AND THE IMPLEMENTATION OF RACISM

The famous arctic researcher Robert Peary brought a group of Pole Eskimos to New York in 1897. The youngest of this group was a child called Minik. The group, which included Minik and his father, were exhibited for a long time at the American Museum of Natural History. During that time, Minik's father lost his life through sickness. Minik remained alone and unprotected in New York. And one day Minik saw that his father's skeleton was being exhibited in the American Museum of Natural History as "an example of the species." Although he asked for his father's body, the museum authorities turned the request down.

Another point worthy of note regarding Minik's life was Robert Peary, the researcher who brought the Eskimos to America, held racist views. Although he lived among the Eskimos, Peary openly thought that these people were not equal to him. According to Peary, Eskimos and Negroes were members of inferior races. Although they were strong, intelligent, and trustworthy people who provided for their families, they were not as good as the white man... One time he wrote the following piece of insolence: "I have often been asked: 'Of what use are Eskimos to the world? They are too far removed to be of any value for commercial enterprises; and, furthermore, they lack ambition. They value life only as does a fox, or a bear, purely by instinct."[1] His purpose in bringing Eskimos to America was explained by a researcher on the subject: "What were Peary's reasons for bringing these six Eskimos to New York? ...Perhaps these six Eskimos were just specimens, much like the skulls and skeletons he had collected earlier, but more interesting because blood still coursed in their veins. ...He had also felt a morbid affinity for the bodies of other Eskimos he knew by name, which he had exhumed the year before from their fresh graves and carted off south to grace the halls of the museum."[2]

Minik, Ota Benga, and many other people whose names are not known, suffered inhuman treatment, in this and other ways, at the hands of so-called 'scientists" who looked on some races as "inferior."

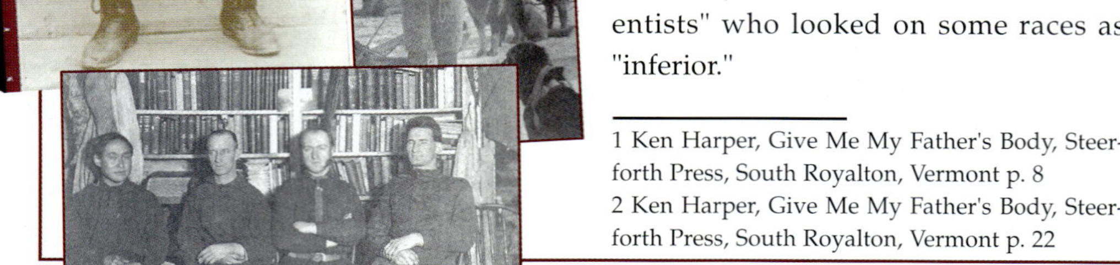

---

1 Ken Harper, Give Me My Father's Body, Steerforth Press, South Royalton, Vermont p. 8
2 Ken Harper, Give Me My Father's Body, Steerforth Press, South Royalton, Vermont p. 22

THE RACIST MENTALITY STILL EXISTS, AND DRAWS STRENGTH FROM DARWIN...

Racist prison murder

By Naema Choudhury

A racist attack left 19-year-old Zahid Mubarek in a fatal coma just hours before he was due to be released. He died of severe head injuries and brain damage. Psychopath, Robert Stewart, was sentenced to life imprisonment at Kingston Crown Court earlier this month. Judge Mr Justice Grigson said, "as you are a danger to yourself and a danger to the public, custody for life is wholly appropriate". Stewart pleaded not guilty and when he was found guilty this was turned against him, he verbally abused the jurors and showed a remorseless 'V' sign to Mubarek family.

Zahid was just hours away from being standing by his victim, holding a table leg in his right hand. Zahid was lying on his blood-soaked bed. Nicholson said, "He looked shell-shocked or something...He said: 'It was an accident Guv'." When asked why he carried out the attack, Stewart simply replied, "Because I felt like it." It was found that Stewart harboured extreme racist viewpoints. In one letter to a friend, Stewart wrote, "I'm going to bomb the Asian community of Great Norbury...it's all about immigrants getting smuggled into here, Romanians, Pakis, Niggers, Chinkies, taking over the country and using us to breed half castes." In a surreal twist, it emerged he had written of murdering his cell-mate. "If I don't get

is the very question posed by Solici for the Mubarek Family, Imran Kha He believes that the institutions volved in this case, Feltham Young (fenders Institution and the Pris Service are not wholly innocent in t matter. Director General of the Pris Service, Martin Narey, said, "Zal Mubarek's murder was a wicked cri by someone whom we now know to b racist." Just how true is this statemen The truth is that prison staff knew ve well that Stewart held extreme rac prejudices, had violent tendencies a displayed unpredictable behaviour - a yet proceeded to place Mubarek in same cell as him. Stewart's prison f showed that he had 19 previous conv

Superiority Comes From Character, Not Blood

Darwin's portraying human beings as a developed species of animal and his presentation of some races as not yet having completed their development, and as species closer to animals was intensely dangerous and destructive in human history. Those who took this claim of Darwin's as their guide mercilessly oppressed other races, forced them to live under the harshest conditions, and even exterminated them.

Bryan Appleyard, author of the book *Brave New Worlds*, explains the tyrannical mentality underlying racism, and the results of it, in this way:

> The point is that once people decide you are a lesser creature for whatever reason, either superstitious or scientific, there appears to be no limit to what cruelty they may inflict on you. And they are likely to inflict that cruelty feeling fully justified, because it is but a small step from believing another human being is inferior to believing that he is bad, dangerous, or threatening to 'superior' beings. Indeed, some may generalize the point even further and insist that all 'inferior' beings are dangerous because they threaten the life or health of the entire human race. They may then advocate sterilization, restrictions on marriage, or even murder to prevent the outcast's assault on the integrity of the species.[42]

All human beings, however, are created the same. Every one was created by Allah (God). The Qur'an announces human beings' creation in this way:

> **He who has created all things in the best possible way. He commenced the creation of man from clay; then produced his seed from an extract of base fluid; then formed him and breathed His Spirit into him and gave you hearing, sight and hearts. What little thanks you show! (Surat al-Sajda: 7-9)**

As the above verses reveal, human beings carry the soul Allah breathed into them. Every human being, with no racial difference, thinks, feels, loves, suffers, feels excitement, and knows love, affection, and compassion. And every human being also knows tyranny, contempt, and difficulty. For this reason, all though history, those who believe people of other races to be semi-developed animals and mistreat them, those who offend, oppress, exploit even one person, and those who support these practices with the false evidence and theories they produced, have committed a great sin in their ignorance.

In our time there exist cultures of relatively undeveloped human societies. These people have all human characteristics, but they lack those criteria which, from technical and cultural aspects, generally rule the world. For reasons of the climate they live in and natural conditions, many communities have lived isolated from general world society and have developed very different cultures. But in each one there exist all the features, customs, and habits common to humanity. Those with hidden agendas, and those who have seen advantage in racism, enthusiastically embraced Darwin's theory and accepted these people, who were no different from other humans, as members of an inferior race and even animals. As a result of this view, even in our day people have emerged who oppress and despise backward people and communities on the grounds they have not evolved sufficiently.

Allah, however, completely forbids racism. Allah created every human being, in different colours and speaking different tongues. This is an indication of the art and variety of Allah's creation:

Among His Signs is the creation of the heavens and earth and the variety of your languages and colours. There are certainly Signs in that for every being. (Surat ar-Rum: 22)

In Allah's sight the only superiority is a person's character, his avoiding all types of sin and rebellion, degeneracy and deviation, and the superior morality deriving from his piety. Apart from his piety no human can have any superiority to any other deriving from any of his features. Allah reveals this in a verse:

Mankind! We created you from a male and female, and made you into peoples and tribes so that you might come to know each other. The noblest among you in Allah's sight is the one with the most piety (who best performs his duty to Allah). Allah is All-Knowing, All-Aware. (Surat al-Hujurat: 13)

THE TERRIBLE ALLIANCE BETWEEN DARWIN AND FASCISM

The Bloody Alliance Between Darwin and Hitler

Nazism was born in the chaos of the Germany which emerged defeated from the First World War. The leader of the party was the angry and aggressive Adolf Hitler. Racism formed the basis of Hitler's world view. Hitler believed that the Aryan race, the fundamental element of the German nation, was superior to all the other races and had to rule them. He dreamed that the Aryan race would found a world empire that would last 1,000 years.

The scientific support Hitler found for these racist theories was Darwin's theory of evolution.

Hitler's most important idea-moulder, the racist German historian Heinrich von Treitschke, was strongly affected by Darwin's theory of evolution and based his racist views on Darwinism. He used to say, **"Nations can only develop by violent competition like Darwin's survival of the fittest,"** and declared that this meant lasting and inevitable war. His view was that, **"Conquering by the sword is a way of bringing civilisation to barbarism and knowledge to ignorance."** He thought: "The yellow races have no understanding of artistic ability and political freedom. **It is the destiny of the black races to serve the whites and to be the target of the whites' loathing for all eternity...**"[43]

While Hitler was developing his theories he drew inspiration, like Treitschke, from Darwin and particularly Darwin's idea of the fight for survival. The title of his notorious book Mein Kampf ("My Struggle") was inspired by the idea of this fight for survival. Just like Darwin, Hitler gave non-European races the status of monkeys, and said, "Take away the Nordic Germans and nothing remains but the dance of apes."[44]

In the 1933 Nuremberg party rally, Hitler proclaimed that "a higher race subjects to itself a lower race… a right which we see in nature and which can be regarded as the sole conceivable right," because it was founded on science.[45]

Hitler, who believed in the superiority of the Aryan race, believed that the superiority of this race was given to it by nature. In *Mein Kampf* he wrote the following:

The Jews formed a sub-human counter race, predestined by their biological heritage to evil, just as **the Nordic race was designated for nobility**… History would culminate in a new millennial empire of unparalleled splendour, based on a new racial hierarchy ordained by nature herself.[46]

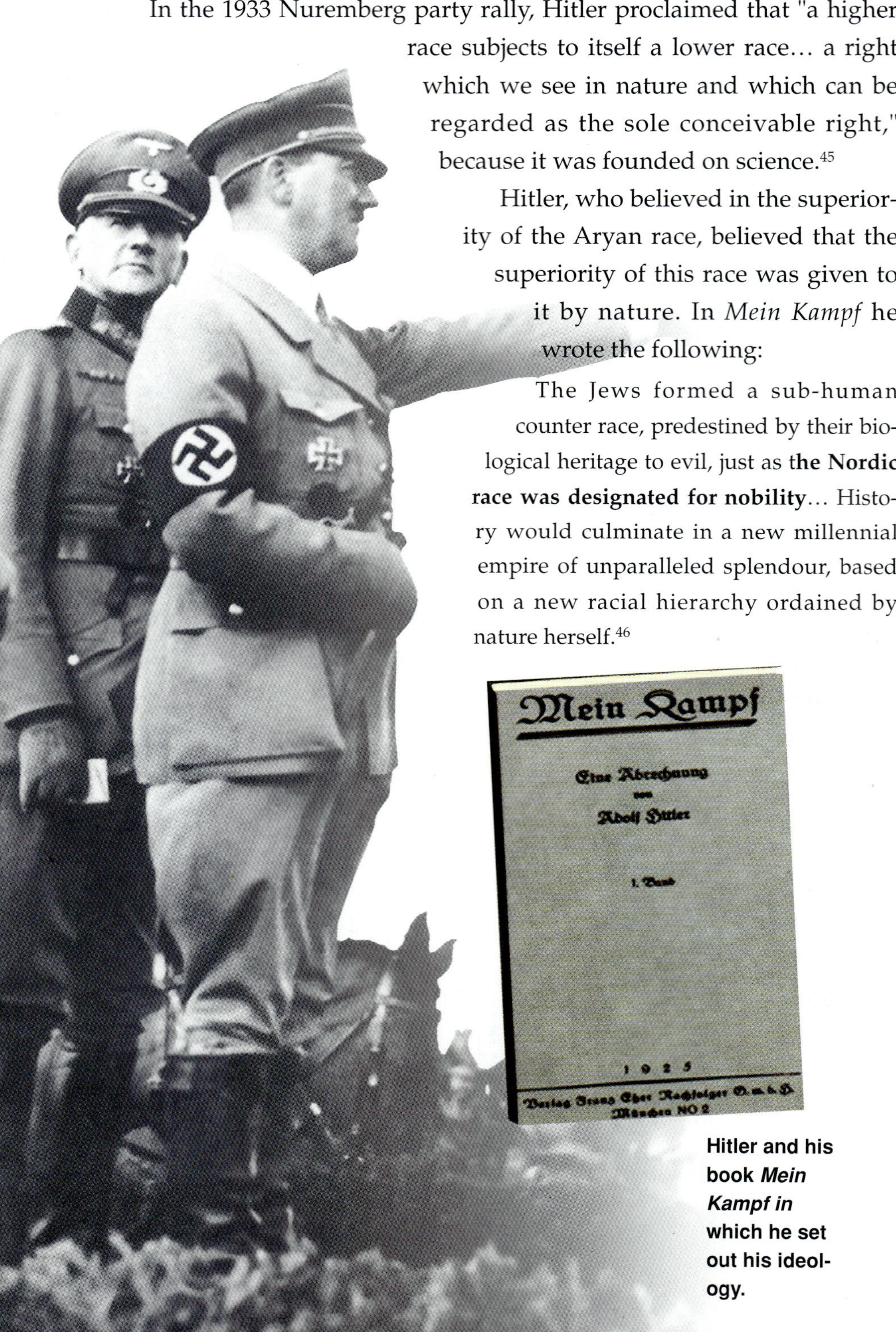

Hitler and his book *Mein Kampf* in which he set out his ideology.

Hitler, who thought that human beings were highly developed animals, believed that instead of allowing natural forces and chance, in a word coincidence, to control evolution, it was necessary to take the management of it into his own hands to develop the human race. And this was the ultimate aim of the Nazi movement. In order to realise this aim, the first step was to separate, to isolate, the inferior races from the Aryan race, the race they believed to be superior.

At this point the Nazis moved to the implementation of Darwinism, and took as their example the "theory of eugenics" which itself had its origins in Darwinism.

The Theory of Eugenics Was Based on Darwin's Ideas

The theory of eugenics, which emerged in the first half of the 20th century, meant the weeding out of sick and handicapped people and the "improving" of the human race by increasing the number of healthy individuals. According to the theory of eugenics, in the same way that better kinds of animals can be produced by mating healthy animals with each other, so the human race could be improved in the same way.

As might be expected, those who put forward the eugenics programme were Darwinists. At the head of the eugenics wave in England came Charles Darwin's cousin, Francis Galton, and his son Leonard Darwin.

It was clear that the idea of eugenics was a natural result of Darwinism. In fact, this truth was awarded special

Francis Galton (left) and Leonard Darwin (right).

importance in those publications which sup-ported eugenics, "Eugenics is man's taking charge of his own evolution," it was said.

Kenneth Ludmerer, a medical historian at Washington University, noted that the idea of eugenics is as old as Plato's *Republic* but he also added that Darwinism was the reason for the rise in interest in the idea in the 19th century:

Ernst Haeckel

> … modern eugenics thought arose only in the nineteenth century. The emergence of interest in eugenics during that century had multiple roots. The most important was the theory of evolution, for Francis Galton's ideas on eugenics–and it was he who created the term "eugenics"–were a direct logical outgrowth of the scientific doctrine elaborated by his cousin, Charles Darwin.[47]

In Germany the first person to be influenced by and to spread eugenics was the famous evolutionary biologist Ernst Haeckel. Haeckel was a close friend and supporter of Darwin. To support the theory of evolution, he put forward the claim "recapitulation," which proposed that the embryos of different living creatures resembled one another. It later emerged that Haeckel had falsified the data when putting forward this claim.

While Haeckel was on the one hand making scientific forgeries of this kind, on the other he was putting forward eugenic propaganda. He suggested that newly-born handicapped children should be killed forthwith and that this would speed up the evolution of society. He went even further, claiming that lepers and people with cancer and mental illnesses should be painlessly killed, or else these people would be a burden on society and would slow down evolution.

The American researcher George Stein summed up Haeckel's blind allegiance to the theory of evolution in an article of his in the magazine

American Scientist in this way:

> ... [Haeckel] argued that Darwin was correct ... humankind had unquestionably evolved from the animal kingdom. Thus, and here the fatal step was taken in Haeckel's first major exposition of Darwinism in Germany, humankind's social and political existence is governed by the laws of evolution, natural selection, and biology, as clearly shown by Darwin. To argue otherwise was backward superstition.[48]

Haeckel died in 1919. But his ideas were inherited by the Nazis. Shortly after Hitler came to power an official eugenics programme was initiated. Hitler summed up the new policy in these sentences:

> In the popular state, the education of the mind and the body will play an important role, but human selection is just as important. ...The state has the responsibility of declaring as unfit for reproductive purposes anyone who is obviously ill or genetically unsound. ... **and must carry through with this responsibility ruthlessly without respect to understanding or lack of understanding on the part of anyone**. ...**Stopping reproduction of the bodily degenerate or psychically ill for a period of only 600 years would lead ...to an improvement in human health which can hardly be envisaged today**. If the fertility of the healthiest members of the race were realized and planned the result would be a race which ... would have lost the

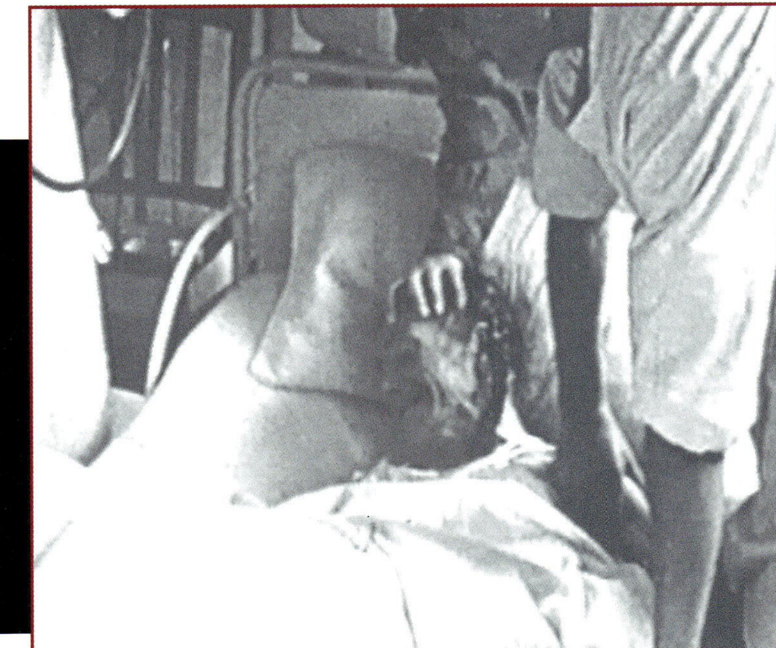

Elderly and sick people killed under Hitler's policy of eugenics.

seeds of bodily and spiritual decay which we now carry. [49]

As a necessity of this policy of Hitler's, the mentally ill, the disabled, the blind from birth, and those with genetic diseases in German society, were rounded up in special "sterilisation centres." These people were regarded as parasites harmful to the purity and evolutionary progress of the German race. A while later in fact, these people who were removed from society **began to be killed by secret order of Hitler.**

These murders were presented as perfectly reasonable and those who were accepted as genetically inferior were described as "unprofitable" and obstacle to the development of the nation. Groups, including various races and peoples, which were seen as inferior races slowly began to be included. Later again sick elderly people, those with jaundice, those with serious mental defects, the deaf and dumb, and even those with fatal diseases were included.

After the black athlete Jesse Owens won four gold medals at the 1936 Berlin Olympics, Hitler, even though he congratulated all the competitors, refused to congratulate Jesse Owens and left the stadium. Some evolutionists even advocated the view that women were evolutionarily inferior

!936 Berlin Olympic Games gold medallist Jesse Owens, who was not congratulated by Hitler because he was black.

Jesse Owens is star of Nazi Games

Aug 16. The Berlin Olympic Games closed with a host of records by the 53 competing nations and 5,000 athletes and must be considered a sporting success, despite the Germans making it clear that their spectacular and highly efficient organisation ultimately had one aim; to glorify the Nazi regime of Adolf Hitler.

The games were awarded to Berlin before Hitler came to full power, and once his dictatorial and racial policies became clear there were moves, particularly in the US with its influential Jewish population, to organise a boycott.

This failed but the Germans, to ward off some of the criticism, selected a few token Jewish competitors in their team. However, in the event it was not the Jews but a Negro, who caused the gravest embarrassment to the Nazis and dogma of Ayrian supremacy.

For the undisputed star of the Games was very much non-Ayrian and very black. The boyish, ever-smiling, ever-modest Jesse Owens destroyed two world-class sprint fields to win the 100 metres and 200 metres; he won the long jump, in one of the greatest field event contests in Olympic history, over the (equally modest and likeable) German Lutz Long; and he took his fourth gold medal leading the United States to a world record in the 400-metre relay.

These victories presented the Nazi regime with a problem. When Hans Woelke won the shotput on the first day Hitler had the champion paraded before him but after Owens' first win Hitler faced the dilemma of recognising him too, or flouting world opinion, and the admiring German crowd, by ignoring him. Propaganda minister Josef Goebbels dubbed Owens and the other American blacks "black mercenaries" but in the end Hitler was persuaded not to appear publicly with the winners.

Even so, when Lutz Long finished second to Owens, Hitler congratulated him privately and ignored Owens. Then after Owens' final 200 metre triumph, while the crowd rose to salute him, Hitler left the stadium.

Owens apart, other notable performances included: the Korean Kitei Son, running reluctantly in the colours of the Japanese Empire, who won the marathon from Britain's Ernie Harper; the British

The poster depicts an Aryan hero.

4 x 400-metre relay squad who brilliantly stole a gold medal from the USA; and, in what many consider to have been the best track race in the 40 years of the modern Olympic Games, New Zealander Jack Lovelock's record win over world record holder Glenn Cunningham (USA) and the reigning Olympic champion Luigi Beccali (Italy) in the 1500 metres.

Jesse Owens runs for another gold at the Games. Hitler refused to even shake his hand, because he was black.

to men. Dr Robert Wartenberg, later a prominent neurology professor in California, tried to prove women's inferiority by arguing that they could not survive unless they were 'protected by men'. He concluded that because the weaker women were not eliminated as rapidly due to this protection, a slower rate of evolution resulted and for this reason natural selection was less operative on women than men. Based on these thoughts, women in Nazi Germany were openly prohibited from entering certain professions.[50]

Following the development of Darwinism and the idea of eugenics, In Germany, "racial scientists" openly advocated the killing of unwanted members and segments of the population. One of these scientists, Adolf Jost, "issued an early call for direct medical killing in a book published in 1895, *Das Recht auf den Tod (The Right to Death)*. Jost argued that **"for the sake of the health of the social organism, the state must take responsibility for the death of individuals."** Adolf Jost was a mentor to Adolf Hitler, who showed himself on the political stage nearly 30 years later. "The state must see to it that only the healthy beget children," Hitler said. "It must declare unfit for propagation all who are in any way visibly sick or who have inherited a disease and can therefore pass it on."[51]

Under a law passed in 1933, 350,000 mentally ill people, 30,000 gypsies, and hundreds

Hitler gathered blonde, blue-eyed German girls in a camp and ensured they would be together with SS officers. In this way he dreamed of building a superior race

of black children were sterilised by such methods as castration, x-rays, injection, and electric shocks to the genital area. One Nazi officer said, "National Socialism is nothing but applied biology."[52]

As well as attempting to hasten the development of the German race by the murder of and ruthless policies directed at innocent people, Hitler was also implementing another condition of eugenics. Blond, blue-eyed men and women, accepted as representative of the German race, were encouraged to form relationships and have children. In 1935 special reproduction farms were established for this purpose. These farms, where young girls conforming to racist criteria were installed, were frequently visited by SS units. The illegitimate children born on these farms were to be raised as the soldiers of the intended 1,000-year German kingdom.

The Nazis' Aryan Racial Aberration

The Nazis again used Darwinist concepts to allegedly prove the superiority of the Aryan race. Darwin had proposed that as people evolved so their skulls grew larger. The Nazis embraced this idea fiercely and set about tak-

THE MASTER RACE DEVIATION

Nazi officers, trained according to evolutionary ideas, sought the master race by measuring skulls, noses, and foreheads.

ing skull measurements to show that the German race was superior. In all corners of Nazi Germany comparisons were made showing that German skulls were larger than those of other races. Teeth, eyes, hair and other features were evaluated with evolutionary measurements. Individuals found not to match up to German race measurements were to be exterminated in the name of the principles of eugenics.

Whenever he holds the upper hand (or he turns his back), he rushes around the earth making mischief therein. He destroys (people's) crops and breeding stock. Allah does not love mischief. (Surat al-Baqara: 205)

Just like Hitler, Heinrich Himmler, the head of the Gestapo, and other Nazi officers held Darwinist views and possessed the racist and ruthless ideas this led to.

All this madness was carried out in the name of implementing Darwinist principles on society. The American historian Michael Grodin, author of the book *The Nazi Doctors and the Nuremberg Code*, reveals the reality in this way:

> I think what happened was that there was a perfect match of Nazi ideology and Social Darwinism and racial hygiene as it developed in the turn of the 20th Century.[53]

George Stein explains the subject

> National socialism, whatever else it may have been was ultimately the first fully self-conscious attempt to organize a political community on a basis of an explicit biopolicy: **a biopolicy fully congruent with the scientific facts of the Darwinian revolution.**[54]

The famous evolutionist Sir Arthur Keith comments on Hitler as follows:

> **The German Führer is an evolutionist;** he has consciously sought to make the practice of Germany conform to the theory of evolution.[55]

The author of the book *Darwin: Before and After*, Robert Clarke, concluded, Adolf Hitler: "...was captivated by evolutionary teaching – probably since the time he was a boy. Hitler reasoned ... that a higher race would always conquer a lower."[53] The political philosophy of Nazi Germany took shape under the influence of these ideas of Hitler's.

The author of the book *Race and Reich*, Joseph Tenenbaum noted that the political philosophy of Germany was built on the belief that critical for evolutionary progress were:

> ... struggle, selection, and survival of the fittest, all notions and observations arrived at ... by Darwin ... but already in luxuriant bud in the German social philosophy of the nineteenth century. ... Thus developed the doctrine of Germany's inherent right to rule the world on the basis of superior strength ... [of a] "hammer and anvil" relationship between the Reich and the weaker nations.[57]

Adolf Hitler was not alone among Nazi leaders in his "war of ideological evolution." Heinrich Himmler, head of the Gestapo, "stated that the law of nature must take its course in the survival of the fittest." In fact, all of the Nazi leaders were committed both to evolution and Germanic racism, as were most German scientists and industrialists during those dark years.[58]

Hitler's Hatred of Religion

Another reason for the great importance Hitler attached to the theory of evolution was his seeing the theory as a weapon against religious belief. Hitler had a great hatred of divine religions. Moral virtues such as compassion, mercy, and humility, ordered by divine religions, represented a great obstacle to the ruthless and warrior Aryan type the Nazis wanted to create. For this reason, once the Nazis came to power in 1933 they tried to turn German society back to its old pagan beliefs. The swastika, a symbol from the old pagan cultures, was a sign of this return. The Nazi ceremonies held in every corner of Germany were a return to the ancient pagan rites. The idea of evolution, an inheritance from pagan cultures, fitted in exceedingly well with the ideology of Nazism for this reason. Hitler once revealed his attitude toward Christianity when he bluntly stated that religion is an:

> ...organized lie [that] must be smashed. The State must remain the absolute master. When I was younger, I thought it was necessary to set about [destroying religion] ...with dynamite. I've since realized there's room for a little subtlety .... The final state must be ... in St. Peter's Chair, a senile officiant; facing him a few sinister old women... The young and healthy are on our side ... Our peoples had previously succeeded in living all right without this religion. I have six divisions of SS men absolutely indifferent in matters of religion.[59]

Daniel Gasman revealed the reasons for Hitler's hatred of religion in his book *The Scientific Origins of National Socialism*:

> Hitler stressed and singled out the idea of biological evolution as the most foremost weapon against traditional religion and he repeatedly condemned Christianity for its opposition to the teaching of evolution... For Hitler, evolution was the hallmark of modern science and culture.[60]

Actually, the fundamental cause of the countless catastrophes visited upon the world in the 20th century was the character of such people as Hitler and the Nazis who had no religion. These people who denied the existence of God and believed that human beings had evolved to become developed animals, saw themselves as unchecked, with no responsibility to answer to anyone. Because they had no fear of God and the hereafter they knew no limit to their immorality and tyranny, and for that reason they mercilessly killed millions of people. The difficulties and pains there

Nazi gatherings resembled ancient pagan ceremonies.

will be in a society without religion are clearly to be seen in the example of Hitler. And not just Hitler: as we shall see later Stalin, Mao, Pol Pot, Franco, Mussolini and the others who drowned the 20th century in blood were known for being completely devoid of religion. A lesson must of course be drawn from the nightmare which comes from lack of religion.

Whereas those who fear Allah and live by Qur'anic morality always bring peace, calm, security, plenty, and enlightened times to a society. People faithful to the religion of Allah never disturb the peace anywhere in the world, on the contrary they always encourage compassion, pity, friendship, faithfulness, and co-operation.

The swastika Hitler used was a symbol belonging to old pagan cultures.

Photographs showing the state of the people during the Second World War.

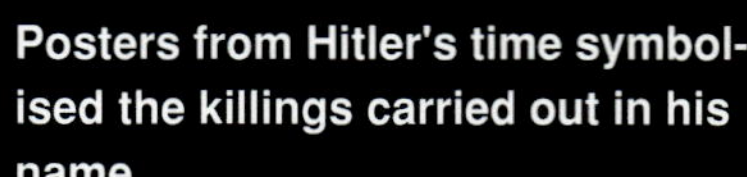

Posters from Hitler's time symbolised the killings carried out in his name.

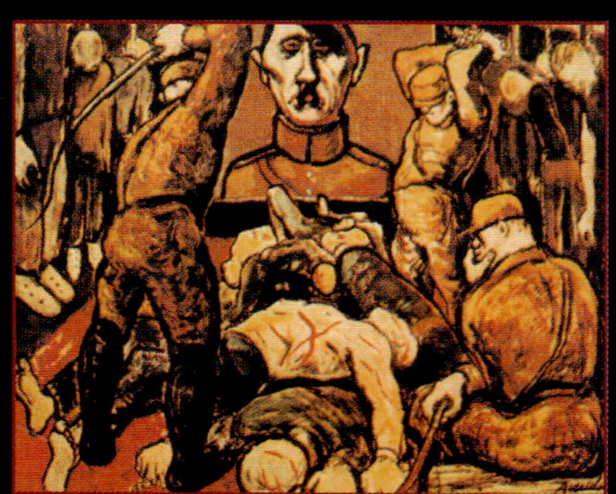

Hitler was the cause of the killing of millions of people, and for millions being left homeless and alone. His inhuman ideology was based on Darwin's theses of superior and inferior races. And he did not hesitate to kill those he saw as inferior races.

These pictures sum up the suffering, fear, terror, and anguish that Hitler and those who shared his views inflicted on humanity. Darwinism, which was the ultimate source of this nightmare, still continues to inflict suffering on mankind all over the world.

The Catastrophes Brought About by the Darwinist-Fascist Mussolini

In the same way that Hitler determined his policy by employing Darwinism, so his contemporary and ally Benito Mussolini made use of Darwinist claims and concepts to set Italy on imperialist and Fascist foundations.

Mussolini was a thorough Darwinist, who believed that violence had been a propelling force in history and that war led to revolution. For him, "the reluctance of England to engage in war only proved the evolutionary decadence of the British Empire."[61]

At the head of the magazine *The People of Italy (Il Popolo d'I-talia)*, which he founded with financial assistance from the French government, he put the phrase, "He who has iron will also have bread." In other words he was telling the people that in order to be able to fill their stomachs they needed the power to wage war.

Mussolini chose the axe as the symbol of Fascism and the

Fascist Party. Because the axe was the symbol of war, violence, death, and massacre.

Mussolini's conduct, aggressive and prone to violence like every Fascist, is described in Denis Mack Smith's book. In his book, Smith stated that one of Mussolini's unchanging beliefs was aggression and his fundamental instinct was to resort to violence.[62]

Like the other Darwinist-Fascists, Mussolini's warlike, aggressive and oppressive policies led to many people being massacred, being left without home and family, and to the country's being left in ruins. Violence and oppression were practised, by means of the Blackshirts, not only in his own country, but in others too. In 1935 he occupied Ethiopia, and by 1941 had had 15,000 people wiped out. He did not delay in backing and justifying his occupation of Ethiopia with Darwinism's racialist views. According to Mussolini the Ethiopians were inferior because they were of the black race, and being governed by a superior race like the Italians should have been an honour for them.

Mussolini's murder squads, the Blackshirts.

On the other hand he continued the oppression of the Muslims which had begun with Italy's occupation of Libya on Oct. 3, 1911, and actually increased the attacks aimed against Muslims. The occupation only came to an end with Mussolini's death in an agreement made on Feb. 10, 1947. During that period 1.5 million Muslims were martyred and hundreds of thousands wounded.

Mussolini, who has gone down in history for his ruthlessness and oppression, described the Fascism which he supported and put into practice in a speech:

> Fascism is no longer liberation but tyranny, no longer the safeguard of the nation but the defense of private interests.[63]

As we have seen in the examples from Hitler and Mussolini, Fascism, where the strong and cruel were right and superior and where the only way to success and development was brute force, aggression, violence, and war, was an implementation of Darwin's claims that "The strong live, the weak die," and led to suffering for millions.

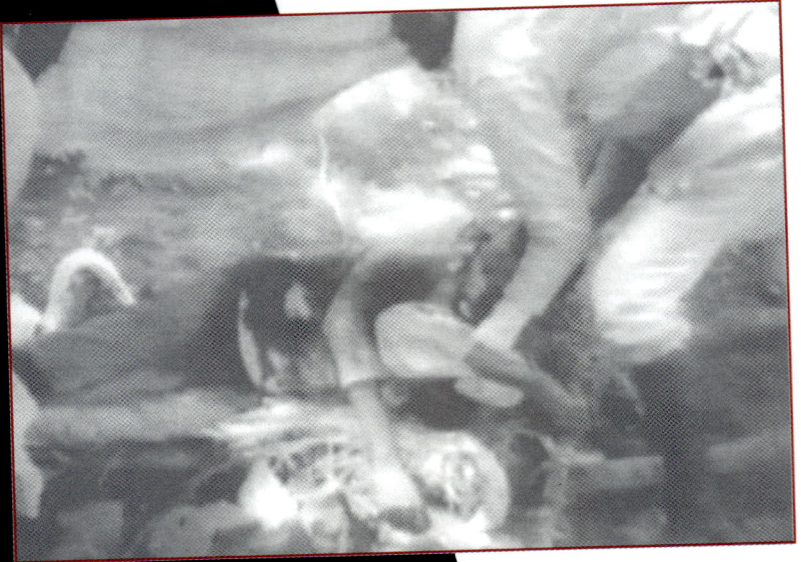

Pictures of the Ethiopian people, oppressed by Mussolini.

A member of Parliament who spoke against Mussolini was kidnapped and murdered in broad daylight. The picture shows the removal of the MP's body from the forest where it was later found.

The Fascist Franco and the Oppression He Gave Rise to in Spain

Another of the Fascist oppressors who turned the 20th century into a lake of blood was Franco. He organised the "Falange" movement in Spain with the support of the Darwinist Fascists Hitler and Mussolini, and brought great suffering and oppression to the people of Spain. Franco dragged his people into civil war, turning brother against brother, father against son.

During the Spanish Civil War an average of 250 people a day were killed in Madrid, 150 in Barcelona, and 80 in Seville. Some executions were carried out by driving nails into peoples' heads. Pitiless massacres took place all over the country. In a little mountain village to the north of Madrid, for example, 31 villagers were arrested because they had not voted for Franco, and of these 13 were taken out of the village by lorry and killed by the side of the road. The Fascists entered a town with a population of 11,000 near Seville and killed more than 300 people. As a result of the violent events which went on in this way some 800,000 people were killed in the civil war, and 200,000 more executed by order of Franco. Millions were injured or crippled.

Franco Gave Hitler the Population of An Entire Village to Test His Weapons On!

The greatest supporters of the Fascist Franco in the Civil War were Hitler and Mussolini. Franco did not leave his allies' support unrewarded: he made one of the cruellest and most ruthless agreements in history, giving small towns such as Guernica to the Nazis as a gift for them to test their new weapons on.

On the morning of May 5, 1937, the people of the small town of Guernica awoke to the death brought by giant bomber planes and tons of bombs, the new miracles of Nazi technology. The little town had been abandoned by Franco to the Nazi plane tests.[64]

This event was only one of the products of this twisted philosophy which regarded human beings as laboratory animals. This philosophy, which left thousands of people to die just in order to test the power of its weapons and which crippled, injured, and tortured thousands of others, still lives today under different guises. This will continue for as long as Darwinist philosophy and similar oppressions which see human beings as a species of animal and war as the most effective means of progress are kept alive.

There was no mercy even for children in the Spanish Civil War, of which Franco was the cause. People were taken out of their houses for no reason and shot. Innocent people were killed, crippled, and lost their families and loved ones. These were all reflections of Fascist ruthlessness in daily life.

Darwinism's Preparatory Role in the First and Second World Wars

In his book Europe Since 1870 the famous British professor of history James Joll explains one of the factors leading to the outbreak of the First World War as being the belief of the leaders of Europe of the time in Darwinist ideas:

> We have seen how Darwinian ideas had a great influence on the ideology of imperialism at the end of the nineteenth century, but it is important to realise how literally the doctrine of the struggle for existence and of the survival of the fittest was taken by the majority of the leaders of Europe in the years preceding the First World War. The Austro-Hungarian chief of staff for example, Franz Baron Conrad von Hoetzendorff, wrote in his memoirs after the war:

> Philanthropic religions, moral teachings and philosophical doctrines may certainly sometimes serve to weaken mankind's struggle for existence in its

Left page. The situation in London, bombed by German planes in the Second World War.

crudest form, but they will never succeed in removing it as a driving motive of the world… It is in accordance with this great principle that the catastrophe of the world war came about as the result of the motive forces in the lives of states and peoples, like a thunderstorm which must by its nature discharge itself."

Seen against this sort of ideological background, Conrad's insistence on the need for a preventive war in order to preserve the Austro-Hungarian monarchy becomes comprehensible.

We have seen too how these views were not limited to military figures, and that Max Weber for example was deeply concerned with the international struggle for survival. Again Kurt Riezler, the personal assistant and confidant of the German chancellor Theobald von Bethmann-Hollweg, wrote in 1914: "Eternal and absolute enmity is fundamentally inherent in relations between peoples; and the hostility which we observe everywhere… is not the result of a perversion of human nature but is the essence of the world and the source of life itself."[65]

Friedrich von Bernhardi, a First World War general and German Social Darwinist, was also one of these leaders. "War" declared Bernhardi "is a biological necessity"; it "is as necessary as the struggle of the elements of nature"; it "gives a biologically just decision, since its decisions rest on the very nature of things."[66]

The wars of the 20th century visited great destruction on people.

As we have seen, the First World War emerged because of the European thinkers, generals, and leaders who saw waging war, spilling blood, suffering, and inflicting suffering as a kind of "development" and an immutable law of nature. The ideological inspiration which dragged this whole generation to ruin with these completely false ideas was none other than Darwin's concepts of "struggle for life" and "favoured races." Two years after Bernardi said those words, the First World War, which was to bring about biological development (!) began, leaving behind it 8 million dead, hundreds of cities in ruins, and millions of wounded, crippled, homeless and unemployed. The roots of the Nazi war, which started 21 years later and left some 50 million dead, also lie in Darwinism.

Hitler often used to link his policies of war and genocide to Darwinism. He saw war as not only for eliminating weaker races, but also as a force for disposing of weaker mem-

bers of the master race. Nazi Germany praised war partly for this reason, because in their twisted thinking war was an essential step for the progress of the race.

The evolutionist A. E. Wiggam explained "the belief that war develops men," on which Hitler based his policy, in a book published in 1922:

> ... at one time man had scarcely more brains than his anthropoid cousins, the apes. But, by **kicking, biting, fighting ... and outwitting his enemies and by the fact that the ones who had not sense and strength enough to do this were killed off, man's brain became enormous** and he waxed both in wisdom and agility if not in size ....[67]

Hitler drew support from evolutionists such as Wiggam and saw war as an obligation for those who wished to survive. He stated this openly in *Mein Kampf*:

> The whole world of Nature is a mighty struggle between strength and weakness–an eternal victory of the strong over the weak. There would be nothing but decay in the whole of nature if this were not so. He who would live must fight. He who does not wish to fight in this world where permanent struggle is the law of life, has not the right to exist. To think otherwise is to "insult" nature. Distress, misery and disease are her rejoinders.[68]

With the Darwinists' claims that the strong remained after the fight for survival and that species developed by this means being adapted to

human societies, wars also began to be viewed as a necessity for the development of mankind. For example, Hitler ascribed Germany's greatness to the elimination by war of its weaker members over the centuries. Although the Germans were no strangers to war this new "scientific" justification was a force to back up their warlike policies.

Elsewhere, Hitler had claimed, **"human civilization as we know it would not exist if it were not for constant war"**[69]

Haeckel proposed, on the subject of war, that the savage methods of the Spartans, one of the city states that made up Ancient Greece, should be implemented. He wrote that "by killing all but the 'perfectly healthy and strong children' the Spartans were 'continually in excellent strength and vigor'."[70]

War was viewed as "an indispensable regulator" of populations all over Europe, and not just in Germany. "If it were not for war," German Social Darwinist Friedrich Von Bernhardi writes, "we should probably find that inferior and degenerate races would overcome healthy and youthful

Darwinist dictators and despots, who believed that war would lead to progress for mankind, turned the 20th century into a lake of blood. They spread oppression to all corners of the world.

ones by their wealth and their numbers. The generative importance of war lies in this, that it causes selection, and thus war becomes a biological necessity."[71]

As we have seen from our account so far, Hitler and the Nazi ideologues who supported him saw war as a necessity with the inspiration they drew from Darwinism. And by implementing this necessity they visited various miseries on their own people, and on the other peoples of the world. From this point of view it will therefore be absolutely correct to identify Charles Darwin as one of those primarily responsible for the sufferings experienced in World War II.

Professor Dr. Jerry Bergman demonstrates the effect of Darwinism on the Second World War:

> The evidence is very clear that Darwinian ideas had a tremendous impact on German thought and practice... In fact, Darwinian ideas had a tremendous influence on causing WWII, the loss of 40 million lives, and the waste of about 6 trillion dollars. Firmly convinced that evolution was true, Hitler saw himself as the modern savior of humankind... By breeding a superior race, the world would look upon him as the man who pulled humanity up to a higher level of evolution.[72]

Of course there had been countless wars in the world before Darwin put his theory forward. But due to the effects of his theory, war was for the first time given a false approval by science. Max Nordau drew attention to Darwin's negative role in the subject of wars in an article called *The Philosophy and Morals of War*, which made waves in America:

> **The greatest authority of all the advocates of war is Darwin.** Since the theory of evolution has been promulgated, they can cover their natural barbarism with the name of Darwin and proclaim the sanguinary instincts of their inmost hearts as the last word of science.[73]

It was no coincidence that the 20th century should see the bloodiest wars the world has known, coming as it did after the 19th century, which was formed by the ideas of such materialist ideologues as Darwin, Marx, and Freud. Darwinism had prepared the theoretical and so-called scientific ground which would end in war, and the despots who saw war as indispensable for the growth of humanity killed a total of 60 million people in both world wars.

Wars All Over the World

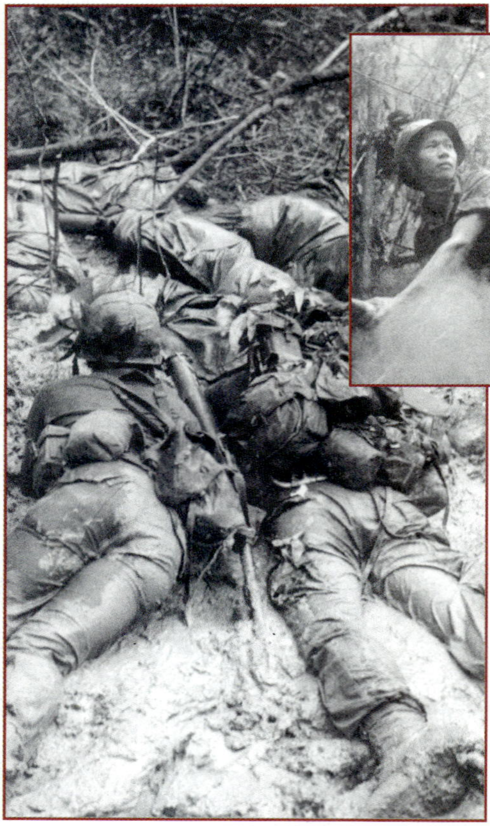

THE VIETNAM WAR

The Vietnam War, in which more than a million people were killed or wounded on both sides, left many suffering people in its wake. Furthermore, many of these people were made to wage war thousands of miles away from their homes.

A father showing South Vietnamese troops his child, who was killed as government forces pursued Viet Cong guerrillas.

There are only grounds against those who wrong people and act as tyrants in the earth without any right to do so. Such people will have a painful punishment. (Surat ash-Shura: 42)

BOSNIA AND KOSOVO

The recent experiences in Bosnia and Kosovo must never be forgotten. The lack of sympathy for innocent people killed because they were Muslims or from a different culture or race, the failure to extend a helping or compassionate hand, and the oppression of innocent people in the middle of Europe for years openly reveal the dominant immorality and lack of compassion in the 20th century.

THE KOREAN WAR

The Korean War, fought between 1950 and 1953, brought great harm to innocent people, the elderly, and children. Human beings grew cruel enough to rain bombs down on innocent people without batting an eye.

JAKARTA

During the May uprising in Jakarta the city morgue was full of dead. In the fighting which went on in the country cities were ruined and cars set on fire.

NORTH IRELAND

Broken people living in fear and poverty, and streets ruined as a result of terrorist attacks in the decades-long clashes between Great Britain and the Irish Republican Army.

The top picture shows the situation in 1972; the picture to the side that in 1986.

LIBERIA

Frequently witnessed scenes of violence in the domestic clashes.

The Neo-Nazis

Even though Fascist leaders such as Hitler and Mussolini, and the Nazi organisations linked to them (the SA, the SS, the Gestapo) or Mussolini's "Blackshirts" today seem like a thing of the past, Neo-Nazi organisations which follow their ideas are still active. In recent years in particular, racist and Fascist movements have re-awoken in many European countries. At the forefront of these movements come the Neo-Nazis in Germany.

Fascism still survives today. Attacks and breaches of the peace by Neo-Nazi groups, particularly in Germany, frequently appear on the agenda. The Neo-Nazis, who praise Darwin on their web pages, are enemies of the Turks.

The Neo-Nazis consist of unemployed hooligans, drug addicts, and bloodthirsty types, and possess all features of the Fascist mentality. One news article about the Neo-Nazis shows how attracted they are to blood and violence:

> Blood, honour, and fanaticism… It is possible to sum up the values of the members of the Fascist Olympia Group in just these three words. Today the organisation has 35,000 members. And in all their eyes can be seen the inordinate desire to rise.[74]

The Neo-Nazis have been influenced by the same Darwinist understanding as their "greats," Hitler and the other Nazi leaders. On the Internet pages which they set up for Nazi and racist propaganda it is possible to come across Darwin's words and praise for Darwin, because Darwin gives support to all the Neo-Nazis' movements and ideas. In their pages, therefore, they put Darwinism forward as a theory which must be accepted, without feeling the need for any evidence.

The attacks and murders the Neo-Nazis carry out are completely ruthless. Neo-Nazis take pleasure in burning people to death, frightening them, and torturing little children, and Turks are one of their main targets. Neo-Nazis reveal their hatred and enmity of Turks in every corner of their Internet sites, and show this hatred in action. This statement about Turks appeared in one Neo-Nazi site:

> For instance, if it were in my power today, I would like to see a large part of the Turks in gas chambers.[75]

The name the Neo-Nazis base their enmity of the Turks on is once again Charles Darwin. The Neo-Nazis think they are providing a so-called scientific explanation for their hatred of Turks by making extracts from Darwin's false and unintelligent claims regarding them. On the last page of this chapter you can see some Neo-Nazi Internet sites which praise Darwin and show the kind of things they have to say about the Turkish nation.

Neo-Nazi violence against Turks and other peoples has recently been on the rise. The Turkish daily *Sabah* dated August 12, 2000 gave a list of

Neo-Nazi attacks during the summer of 2000:

- In June, the windows of the El Rahman Mosque in the town of Gera in the state of Thüringen were broken.

- Two molotov cocktails were thrown at a Turkish mosque in the small town of Eppingen in the state of Baden-Württemberg.

- A molotov cocktail was thrown at the Green Mosque in the Utersen quarter of Pinneberg.

- A building lived in by Turks was set fire to in Memingen.

- In Bocholt a Turkish café and a building lived in by Lebanese were set on fire. Fourteen people were wounded, one seriously.

- In the East German town of Chemnitz the seven-month-old baby of an Iraqi family was thrown to the ground. The baby's face was injured when it hit the concrete.[76]

There were much nastier incidents in the recent past. Taking Darwin's enmity of the Turks as their guide, the Neo-Nazis organised an attack on Turks in Möln in November 1992. Later, in 1993, five Turks were burned by Neo-Nazis in Solingen.[77] The press described this attack as, "The bloodiest racist attack in German history since the Nazi era." Attacks of this kind were often seen in the years that followed. Fires were started in Turks' homes, Turks were beaten and injured. As well as in Germany, similar attacks took place in Holland. In one attack directed at Turks a

Neo-Nazis carried out an attack aimed at Turks in the town of Möln in 1992.

woman and her five children were killed. People who took part in the mourning march that was held received threatening letters with swastikas on.

These incidents are just a few of the racist attacks against Turks. Attacks and murders by these Fascist groups, the inheritors of Darwin and Fascists such as Hitler, still continue. Legal measures will not be enough to stop these inhuman groups' attacks. The sure way to put an end to them is to wage a serious ideological war alongside the legal measures. The outrages perpetrated by these people who see racism as a law of nature will not come to an end so long as Darwinist ideas are not knocked down as science.

Neo-Nazi Internet pages. In these pages Neo-Nazis, who praise Darwin, aim insults and threats at Turks.

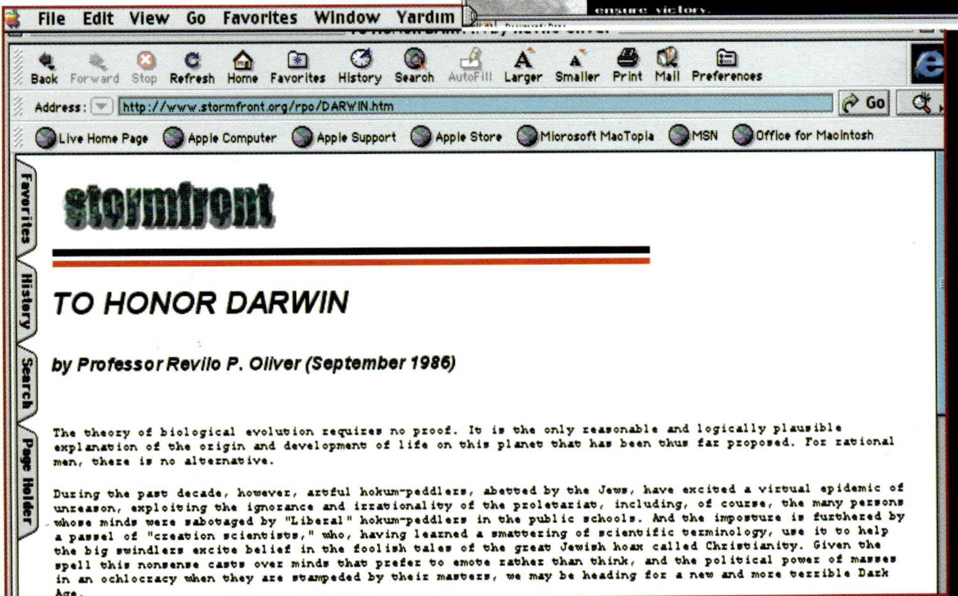

Der 20jährige Thorsten Sempert aus Rostock feuert aus seiner Schreckschußpistole auf Polizisten. Die Waffe hatte er sich eine in Hamburg besorgt. Schon vor Tagen hatte der Zeitschriftenwerber in Rostock Ausländer verprügelt. »Jetzt sind Wohnungen frei kommentierte er zynisch die ausgebrannten Räume des Asylbewerberheims in Lichtenhagen

Deutschland im Herbst

Sind sie die Stimme der schweigenden Mehrheit? Rechtsradikale Jugendliche treten immer aggressiver auf

Tagtäglich werden Asylbewerberheime mit Steinen und Brandbomben angegriffen. In der Bevölkerung machen sich Zukunftsangst und Ausländerfeindlichkeit breit. Politiker taktieren hilflos. Im Ausland wächst die Sorge über den Rechtsruck in Deutschland. Wohin treibt dieses Land?

Stern (No:40/1992) reads:
GERMANY IN FALL
Every day sees attacks on refugee camps with stones and fire-bombs. Popular hatred of foreigners is growing and fear for the future rules. Politicians are helpless. The right-wing movement in Germany is observed with anxiety from abroad. Where is the country headed?

blank-cartridge gun into the air. Two climbed on the bus behind him. When the bus arrived at the training center, they grabbed Mohammed and beat him. One held him while the other pounded him with his fists. When he fell to the ground, he was repeatedly kicked in the face with their steel-toed army combat boots

"I wasn't surprised about the attack," says Mohammed, whose injured face required extensive surgery. "I'm often harassed and called names. But it was the first time that I was beaten up and I've been afraid ever since. When I see the *Glatzen*—the 'bald-heads'—I look around for other people so there'll be witnesses if they attack me. Though I'm not sure they'd help me. Nobody came to my rescue when I was beaten up at the school." Such incidents are commonplace in Germany's newspapers. What dominates the front page day after day is the stunning price tag on the crusade to bring the east into the German mainstream.

THUGS Some disaffected youths in the east are turning towards xenophobic neo-Nazi groups

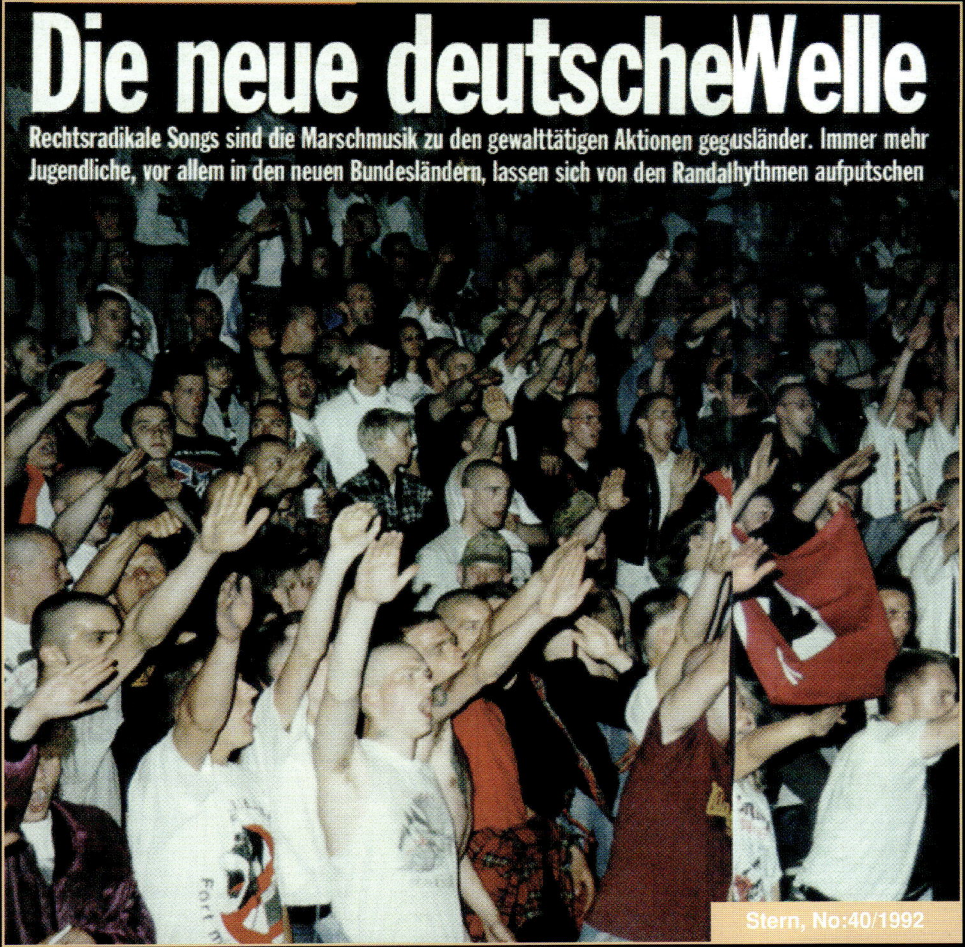
Die neue deutsche Welle
Rechtsradikale Songs sind die Marschmusik zu den gewalttätigen Aktionen gegusländer. Immer mehr Jugendliche, vor allem in den neuen Bundesländern, lassen sich von den Randalhythmen aufputschen
Stern, No:40/1992

Stern (No: 40/1992) reads:

The songs of the radical right form the marching music for violent actions aimed at foreigners. Young people, whose numbers are rising every day, especially in the new German states, are being spurred on by these aggressive rhythms.

ISSUES IN FOCUS
NEO-NAZIS
A GROWING THREAT
KATHLYN GAY

HASS
Wir sind RECHTSRADIKAL und stolz darauf !
Stern, No:30/1999

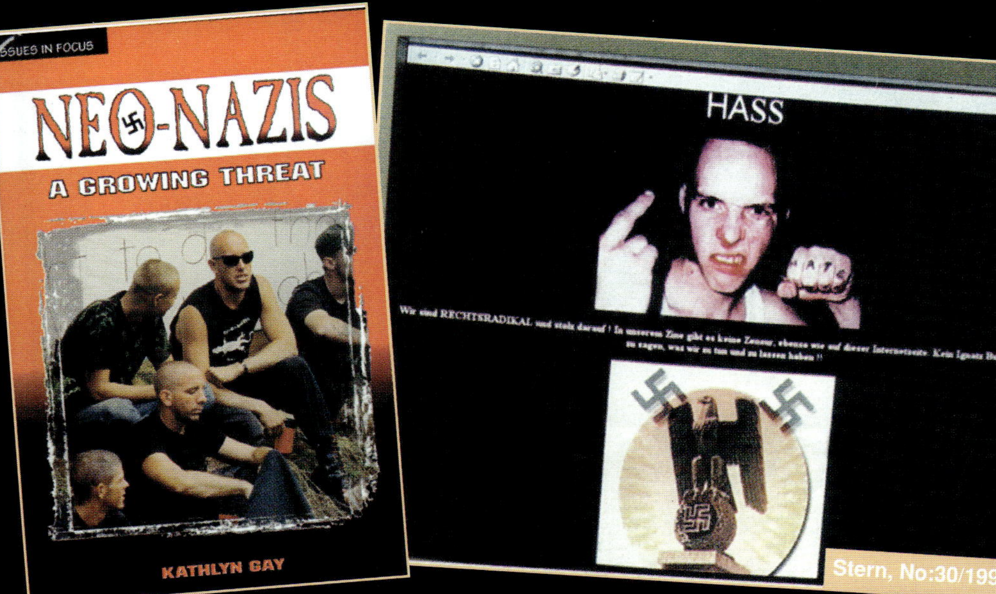

PART 4

DARWINISM: THE SOURCE OF COMMUNIST SAVAGERY

The ideology which brought the greatest harm to mankind in the violence and savagery-filled century we have just left behind, and the most widespread in the world, was without doubt Communism. Communism, which reached its historical peak with the two German philosophers Karl Marx and Friedrich Engels in the 19th century, spilt so much blood in the world that it left even the Nazis and the imperialists behind. It led to the deaths of innocent people and spread violence, fear, and hopelessness among mankind. Even today when someone speaks of The Iron Curtain countries and Russia, images rise up of communities ruled by darkness, fog, and hopelessness, lifeless streets, trouble and fear. No matter how much Communism is thought of as having been torn down in 1991, the debris it left behind it still exists. No matter how "liberalised" one part of the "unrepentant" Communists and Marxists may be, materialist philosophy, the dark side of Communism and Marxism and which turned people away from religion and morality, still continues to influence these people.

This ideology which spread terror to every corner of the world actually represented an idea which goes back to ancient times. Dialectics was a belief that all development in the universe arose as the result of conflict. Based on this belief Marx and Engels set about analysing the history of the world. Marx claimed that the history of man was one of conflict, that the current conflict was one between workers and capitalists, and that the workers would soon rise up and build a Communist revolution.

The most striking feature of the two founders of Communism was that, like all materialists, they nurtured a great hatred of religion. Marx and Engels were both confirmed atheists and saw the doing away with religious beliefs as essential from the point of view of Communism.

But Marx and Engels lacked one important thing: in order to attract a wider public they needed to give their ideology a scientific appearance. And the dangerous alliance which gave rise to the pain, chaos, mass murders, turning of brother against brother, and separatism of the 20th century emerged at this point. Darwin proposed his theory of evolution in his book *The Origin of Species*. And how interesting it is that the basic claims he put forward were just the explanations Marx and Engels were looking for. Darwin claimed that living things emerged as a result of the "struggle for survival" or "dialectical conflict." Furthermore he denied creation and rejected religious beliefs. For Marx and Engels this was an opportunity not to be missed.

Marx and Engels' Admiration of Darwin

Darwinism was of such great importance to Communism that only months after Darwin's book was published, Engels wrote to Marx, **"Darwin, whom I am just now reading, is splendid."**[78]

The founders of Communism, Karl Marx and Friedrich Engels.

THE COLLAPSE OF THE MARXIST VIEW OF HISTORY

Karl Marx, the founder of Communism, adapted Darwin's ideas, which deeply influenced him, to the dialectic process of history. According to Marx, society went through different phases in history, and the factor which determined these phases was the change in the means of production and production relations. According to this view, the economy determined everything else. History went through evolutionary stages: Primitive society, slave society, feudal society, capitalist society, and the last stage, Communist society.

Yet history itself showed that Marx's proposed evolutionary period possessed no validity. At no time in history has any society been seen which has gone through Marx's proposed evolutionary stages. On the contrary, it is possible to see systems which Marx identified as coming before or after each other at the same time in the same society. While one part of a country is experiencing systems similar to the feudal system, capitalist rules may apply in another region. For which reason there is absolutely no proof that the passage from one system to another follows the evolutionary pattern claimed by Marx and the theory of evolution.

On the other hand, none of Marx's prophecies regarding the future came true. It was realised that Marx's theories were not applicable within 10 years of Marx's death. Marx claimed that one after the other the most developed capitalist nations would undergo Communist revolutions, whereas no such period happened. Lenin, one of Marx's greatest followers, tried to explain why these revolutions had not taken place, and then put forward other prophecies that Communist revolutions would be experienced in Third World countries. Yet all of Lenin's claims were proven untrue by history. In our time the number of countries run under Communism can be counted on the fingers of one hand. Furthermore, Marxism used force in the regions where it came to power, and it came to power not by popular movements, as it claimed, but by dictatorial pressure.

In short, recent history has completely disproved Marxist philosophy's predicted period of historical evolution. Theories such as "the dialectic of history" and "historical evolution" in the many volumes written by materialist ideologues such as Marx and Engels, are just products of fantasy.

Marx wrote back to Engels on December 19, 1860, saying, **"This is the book which contains the basis in natural history for our view."**[79]

In a letter Marx wrote to Lassalle, another socialist friend of his, on January 16, 1861, he said: **"Darwin's book is very important and serves me as a basis in natural science for the class struggle in history."**[80] thus revealing the importance of the theory of evolution for Communism.

Marx revealed his sympathy for Darwin by dedicating his most important work, *Das Kapital*, to him. Darwin's copy of Marx's first volume was inscribed by Marx, describing himself as a "sincere admirer" of the English naturalist.[81]

Engels too admitted his admiration for Darwin elsewhere:

Nature is the test of dialectics, and it must be said... that in the last resort nature works dialectically and not metaphysically... In this connection, **Darwin must be named before all others.**[82]

Engels praised Darwin and Marx as being the same, "Just as Darwin discovered the law of evolution in organic nature, so Marx discovered the law of evolution in human history" he said.[83]

In another of his works, Engels stressed the importance of Darwin's having developed a theory opposed to religion:

He (Darwin) dealt the metaphysical conception of nature the heaviest blow by his proof that the organic world of today — plants, animals, and consequently man too — is the product of a process of evolution going on through millions of years.[84]

As well as this, Engels at once showed how he had accepted Darwin's theory by writing an article titled *"The Part Played by Labour in the Transition from Ape to Man."*

The American researcher Conway Zirckle explains why the founders of Communism immediately accepted Darwin's theory"

Marx and Engels accepted evolution almost immediately after Darwin published *The Origin of Species.* Evolution, of course, was just what the founders of communism needed to explain how mankind could have come into being without the intervention of any supernatural force, and consequently it could be used to bolster the foundations of their materialistic philosophy. In addition, Darwin's interpretation of evolution–that evolution had come about through the operation of natural selection–g**ave them an alternative hypothesis to the prevailing teleological explanation of the observed fact that all forms of life are adapted to their conditions.**[85]

Tom Bethell, of *Harper's Magazine*, explains the fundamental link between Marx and Darwin in the following manner:

> Marx admired Darwin's book not for economic reasons but for the more fundamental one that Darwin's universe was purely materialistic, and the explication of it no longer involved any reference to unobservable, nonmaterial causes outside or 'beyond' it. In that important respect, **Darwin and Marx were truly comrades.**[86]

Today the link between Darwinism and Marxism is an obvious truth accepted by everyone. Biographies of Marx always make this plain. For example, a biography of Karl Marx describes the link in this way:

> "Darwinism presented a whole string of truth supporting Marxism and proving and developing the truth of it. The spread of Darwinist evolutionary ideas created a fertile ground for Marxist ideas as a whole to be taken on board by the working class… Marx, Engels, and Lenin attached great value to the ideas of Darwin and pointed to their scientific importance, and in this way the spread of these ideas was accelerated."[87]

As we have seen, Marx and Engels were delighted to believe that Darwin's concept of evolution formed a scientific support for their own atheist world view. But this delight proved to be premature. The theory of evolution saw wide acceptance because it was proposed in a primitive 19th century scientific environment and was full of errors lacking any sort of scientific proof. Science, which developed in the second half of the 20th century, revealed the invalidity of the theory of evolution. This meant the collapse of Communist and materialist thinking as much as it did of Darwinism. (For further details see *The Evolution Deceit* by Harun Yahya). But because scientists with materialist views knew that the collapse of Darwinism also meant the collapse of their own ideologies they tried all possible methods to conceal Darwinism's collapse from people.

The Admiration of the Followers of Marx and Engels for Darwin

Marx and Engels' followers, who brought about the deaths of millions of people and were the reason for hundreds of millions of others living in pain, fear, and violence, accepted the theory of evolution with great joy and interest.

John N. Moore speaks of the links between evolution and the Soviet leaders who implemented Marx and Engels' ideas in Russia:

> The thinking of the leaders of the USSR is rooted deeply in an evolutionary outlook.[88]

It was Lenin who made Marx's project of Communist revolution come true. Lenin, the leader of the Communist Bolshevik movement in Russia, aimed to bring down the Tsarist regime in Russia by force of arms. The chaos after World War I gave the Bolsheviks the opportunity they had been seeking. With Lenin at their head, the Communists seized power by the use of arms in October 1917. After the revolution Russia was the scene of a bloody three-year civil war between Communists and supporters of the tsar.

Lenin and Trotsky

Like the other Communist leaders, Lenin often stressed that Darwin's theory was the fundamental basis of dialectical materialist philosophy.

One of his statements reveals his view of Darwinism:

Darwin put an end to the belief that the animal and vegetable species bear no relation to one another, except by chance, and that they were created by God, and hence immutable.[89]

Trotsky, counted the most important architect of the Bolshevik revolution after Lenin, again attached great importance to Darwinism. He declared his admiration for Darwin in the following way,

Darwin's discovery is the highest triumph of the dialectic in the whole field of organic matter.[90]

Following Lenin's death in 1924, Stalin, widely regarded as the bloodiest dictator in the history of the world, passed to the leadership of the Communist Party. Throughout his 30 years in power, Stalin would try to prove just what a ruthless system Communism was.

Stalin's first important move was to take over the fields of the peasants who made up 80 percent of the population of Russia in the name of the state. In the name of this policy of collectivisation which was intended to do away with private property, all the Russian villagers' crops were collected by armed officials. As a result these was a terrible famine. Millions of women, children, and the elderly who could find nothing to eat ended their lives writhing in hunger. The death toll in the Caucasus alone was 1 million.

Stalin sent hundreds of thousands of people who tried to resist this policy to Siberia's dreadful labour camps. These camps, where the prisoners were worked to death, became the grave of most of these people. On the other hand tens of thousands of people were executed by Stalin's secret police. Millions of people were forced to migrate to the furthest corners of Russia, including the Crimean and Turkestan Turks.

By these bloody policies Stalin killed some 20 million people. Historians have revealed that this savagery gave him enormous personal pleasure. It gave him great pleasure to sit at his desk in the Kremlin and examine the lists of those who had died in the concentration camps or who had been executed.

Apart from his personal psychological state, the main influence which lead him to become such a ruthless killer was the materialist philosophy he believed in. In Stalin's own words, the fundamental basis of this philosophy was Darwin's theory of evolution. He explained the importance he attached to Darwin's ideas:

There are three things that we do to disabuse the minds of our seminary students. We had to teach them the age of the earth, the geologic origin, and **Darwin's teachings**.[91]

While Stalin was still alive a close childhood friend of his recounted how Stalin had become an atheist in the book *Landmarks in the Life of Stalin:*

At a very early age, while still a pupil in the ecclesiastical school, Comrade Stalin developed a critical mind and revolutionary sentiments. He began to read Darwin and became an atheist.[92]

Stalin, one of the bloodiest names in history, the cause of the killing of tens of millions of people, death from starvation and poverty, and of millions of people being left without homes and jobs.

In the same book, G. Glurdjidze, a boyhood friend of Stalin's relates how Stalin had stopped believing in God and had told him that the reason for this was **Darwin's book**, pressurising him into reading it too.[93]

One important indication of Stalin's blind faith in the theory of evolution was the Soviet education system's rejection of Mendel's genetic laws in the period when he came to power. These laws, which had been accepted by the whole world of science since the start of the 20th century, denied Lamarck's claim that "acquired traits can be passed on to later generations." The Russian scientist Lysenko saw this as a heavy blow to the theory of evolution and at the same time a great danger, and told Stalin his ideas. Stalin was impressed by Lysenko's ideas and made him head of the official scientific associations. Thus genetic science, which had dealt a heavy blow to evolution, was not accepted in any Soviet Union scientific association or school until Stalin's death.

In Stalin's period the Soviet Union had turned into an environment of chaos where for millions of people life was permanently under threat, and where they could be taken away, though innocent of any crime, at any moment, to suffer unimagined torments. Not just Communism, but the history of Fascism, too, is full of such attitudes.

Some commentators on history fall into the error, when evaluating these events, of trying to show that the basic cause of all this savagery and mercilessness was that as people, Lenin, Stalin, Mao, Hitler, and Mussolini had unbalanced and psychopathic natures. What kind of coincidence is it, that the whole world should have fallen into the hands of psychologically unbalanced people at the same time?

It is an obvious and definite truth that these people and ideologies all drank from the same well and that they were all portrayed as justified and the only way by the same source. In short there was another guilty party behind these people. The cause of these inhuman and unbalanced leaders dragging millions along behind them, and which allowed them to commit crimes, was the apparent scientific force and support given to them by materialist philosophy and Darwinism.

Mao Tse Tung: Darwin and Marx's Ambassador to China

While Stalin was running his totalitarian regime, another Communist regime which saw Darwinism as its scientific support was founded in China. The Communists under the leadership of Mao Tse Tung came to power in 1949 after a long civil war. Mao set up an oppressive and bloody regime, just like his ally Stalin, who gave him great support. China became the scene of numberless political executions. In the years ahead, Mao's young militants, known as "Red Guards," would drag the country into an atmosphere of utter terror.

Mao openly announced the philosophical foundation of the system he established by saying, **"Chinese socialism is founded upon Darwin and the theory of evolution."**[94]

Being a Marxist and an atheist and a firm believer in evolutionism himself, Mao mandated that the reading material used in this early day "Great Leap Forward" in literacy would be the writings of Charles Darwin and other materials supportive of the evolution paradigm.[95]

When the Chinese Communists came to power in 1950 they took the theory of evolution as the basis of their ideology. Actually, Chinese intellectuals had accepted the theory of evolution long before:

During the 19th century, the West regarded China as a sleeping giant, isolated and mired in ancient traditions.

Mao Tse Tung

Few Europeans realized how avidly Chinese intellectuals seized on Darwinian evolutionary ideas and saw in them a hopeful impetus for progress and change. According to the Chinese writer Hu Shih (Living Philosophies, 1931), when Thomas Huxley's book *Evolution and Ethics* was published in 1898, it was immediately acclaimed and accepted by Chinese intellectuals. Rich men sponsored cheap Chinese editions so they could be widely distributed to the masses.[96]

So, the people who turned to Communism and lead the Communist revolution were these intellectuals who had been "eagerly influenced" by Darwinist ideas.

It was not hard for China, even with its many deep pantheistic beliefs and history, to enter the pincers of Darwinism and Communism. In an article in the *New Scientist* magazine the Canadian Darwinist philosopher Michael Ruse says, concerning early-twentieth-century China:

> **These ideas took root at once**, for China did not have the innate intellectual and religious barriers to evolution that often existed in the West. Indeed, in some respects, **Darwin seemed almost Chinese!** … Taoist and Neo-Confucian thought had always stressed the "thingness" of humans. Our being at one with the animals was no great shock… Today, the official philosophy is Marxist-Leninism (of a kind). But **without the secular materialist approach of Darwinism (meaning now the broad social philosophy), the ground would not have been tilled for Mao and his revolutionaries to sow their seed and reap their crop.**[97]

As Michael Ruse stated above, with the firm settling of Darwinist ideas, China easily took up Communism. The Chinese people, deluded by Darwinist ideas, stood by and watched all the massacres of Mao Tse Tung, one of the most unrestrained killers in history.

Yet Communism was the cause of guerrilla conflicts, bloody acts of terrorism, and civil war in very many countries, not just in China. Turkey was one of these. In the 1960s and 1970s, groups which took up arms against the state dragged Turkey into a dark atmosphere of terrorism with the dream of making a Communist revolution in the country. After 1980, Communist terrorism joined with the current of separatism and was the cause of the deaths of tens of thousands of Turks and of police and soldiers in the course of their duties.

Communist ideology, which brought bloodshed to the world in this way for 150 years was always side by side with Darwinism. Even today, Communists are the foremost supporters of Darwinism. Whenever one looks at those circles which stubbornly support the theory of evolution, in just about every country, one sees the Marxists in the front ranks. Because as Karl Marx said, the theory of evolution forms the basis of Communist ideology from the natural science aspect and gives Communist lack of religion its most important false scientific backing.

The Basis of the Alliance Between Darwinism and Communism: Hatred of Religion

As explained earlier, the most important reason for the materialists' and Communists' clinging to Darwinism is the apparent support Darwinism gives to atheism. Materialist philosophy had existed throughout history, but until the 19th century most philosophers had been restricted to books of theory. The most important reason for this was that until that time most men of science believed in God and were people who believed in the reality of creation. But in the 19th century materialist philosophy and Darwin's theory began to be implemented in the natural sciences. Darwinism was the greatest basis for the irreligious materialist culture which stamped its mark on the 19th century and which most revealed its effects in the 20th century.

The ideologies born of this materialist culture, as we have been examining, lit the fires of two great world wars, countless civil wars and acts of terrorism, genocide, extermination, and savagery. On account of these catastrophes tens of millions of people lost their lives, and hundreds of millions were shamefully oppressed and had to suffer the worst treatment.

Terrorists influenced by the Darwinist-materialist view, like the animals they claimed to be descended from, went off to the mountains and lived in caves in appalling conditions. They could kill men without a second thought and murder babies, the elderly, and the innocent. Seeing neither themselves nor other people as living things created by God with soul, mind, conscience, and understanding, they did to each other what animals do to animals. Stalin's demolition of dozens of churches and mosques is just one indication of Communism's hatred of religion.

In his book *The Long War Against God*, Henry Morris describes the link in this way:

> In spite of its scientific deficiencies, evolution's alleged scientific character has been used to justify all kinds of ungodly systems and practices. The most successful of these, thus far, seems to be communism, and its adherents all over the world have been deluded into thinking that communism must be true because it is based on the science of evolution. [98]

The enmity Communism and materialism had for religion showed itself in all its violence during the Bolshevik uprising. Churches and mosques were razed, and among the categories of those pushed outside the "new socialist society," men of religion had an important place. Despite the fact that most of society was religious people, they were obstructed

from carrying out their religious duties. In order to take Sundays, when Christians went to church, out of the equation, the concept of a common day of rest was removed. Everyone would work five days, but the day of rest could be any day. This measure was deliberately introduced by the communists "to facilitate the struggle to eliminate religion".[99] Following that, in 1928 and 1930 the taxes paid by men of religion were raised by 10 times, their food coupons were taken from them, and they could no longer use the health services, which meant they no longer enjoyed any civil rights, they were often arrested, moved from their posts and sent into exile. By 1936 some 65 percent of mosques and 70 percent of churches had been destroyed.

Some of the most violent measures against religion were taken in Albania. The Communist leader of Albania, known for having no religion, was Enver Hodja, who in 1967 proclaimed Albania the first "religionless" country. Men of religion would be taken into custody for no reason, and some of them were killed while in custody. In 1948 two bishops and 5,000 men of religion were shot. Muslims were killed in the same way. The literary monthly *Nendori* announced that 2,169 mosques and churches had

During and after the Bolshevik revolution there were many attacks on religion. Churches and mosques were pulled down. Works of art in churches were plundered, as can be seen in the above pictures.

been closed down, of which 327 were Catholic places of worship.

The reason for all these practices was, without the shadow of a doubt, Communism's aim of forming societies which would blindly deny the existence of God, had nothing to do with religion, and which only believed in and valued material things. Actually, that was one of Communism's main targets, because the Communist leaders knew that they could only govern as they wished people who had become like machines, and insensitive, unfeeling, and most important of all, non-god-fearing societies, and that they could make them carry out as many killings and as much oppression as they wanted. The claims of Darwinism, which gave support to atheism and which justified all kinds of oppression, cruelty, conflict, and killing, forbidden in religi-

Who could do greater wrong than someone who bars access to the mosques of Allah, preventing His name from being remembered in them, and goes about destroying them? Such people will never be able to enter them – except in fear. They will have disgrace in this world and in the hereafter they will have a terrible punishment. (Surat al-Baqara: 114)

on, encouraged in this way all the ideologies which spilt blood and counted human life as valueless in the 20th century. That is why the last century was full of ceaseless wars, massacres, rebellions, acts of violence, fighting, and enmity.

The Oppression and Violence Inflicted On the World by Darwinist Communists

Anarchy and terror are two of Marxism and Communism's indispensable tools. Marxism's tendency towards terrorism and violence appeared in the experiment of the Paris Commune while Marx was still alive. In particular, terrorism became an indispensable part of Communist ideology with Lenin, while he was making Marx's theory a practicality. Communists spilt the blood of millions of people in every part of the world, and made people undergo pain, fear, and violence by establishing terrorist organisations. As will be seen in the pages that follow, today all the Communist leaders are remembered for the oppression and killings they carried out. Yet despite this some circles still cover their walls with pictures of these pitiless, bloody-handed assassins, and still accept these sadistic people as their teachers.

No matter how much some Communists claim that violence and terrorism are not Communist practices and that they only took place in some individuals' applications of Communism, and no matter how much they try to whitewash Communism, there is an undeniable truth: **The founders of Communism personally defended violence and terrorism and saw them as essential to their ideology.** The American political scientist Samuel Francis has this to say on the subject:

> **Marx and Engels** were generally specific in insisting that revolution will always be violent and that revolutionaries must use violence against the rulers, and in some instances **they did express support of terrorism.**[100]

Karl Marx said "insurrection is an art quite as much as war" and took these words of Danton, one of the foremost names in "revolutionary politics" as a principle, "de l'audace, de l'audace, encore de l'audace" (Attack, attack, and attack again!)[101] There are clear statements by Lenin regarding the

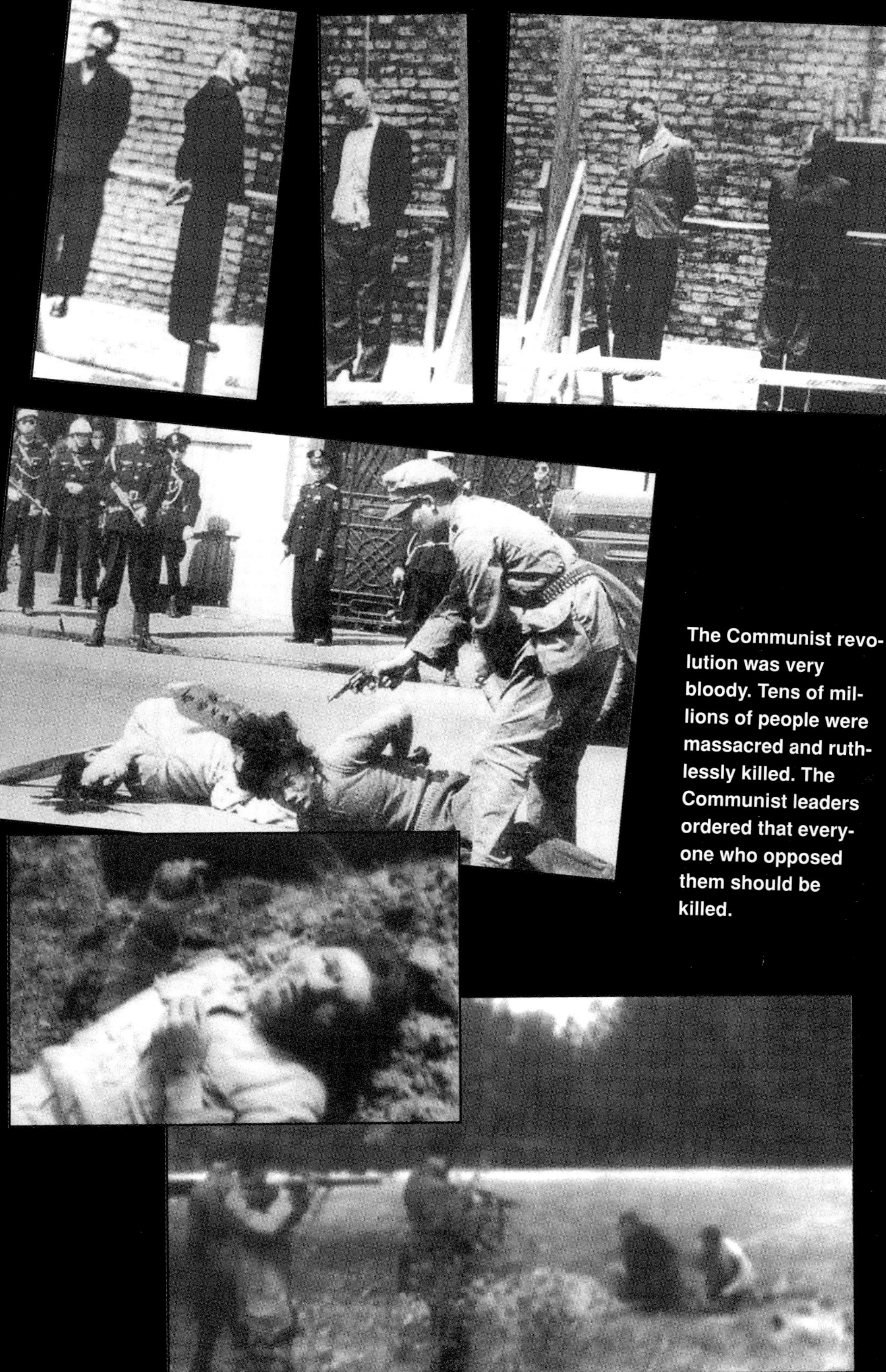

The Communist revolution was very bloody. Tens of millions of people were massacred and ruthlessly killed. The Communist leaders ordered that everyone who opposed them should be killed.

necessity of systematically using terrorism. Here are a few of them:

> In reality the state is nothing but a machine for the suppression of one class by another. Dictatorship is rule based directly on force and unrestricted by laws... The revolutionary dictatorship of the proletariat is rule won and maintained through the use of violence by the proleteriat against the bourgeoisie, rule that is unrestricted by any laws.[102]

> **We are not at all opposed to political killing...** Only in direct, immediate connection with the mass movement can and must individual terrorist acts be of value.[103]

> To become a power the class-conscious workers must win the majority to their side. As long as no violence is used against the people there is no other road to power.[104]

Speaking at a workers' meeting, Lenin gave a terrifying statement of how indispensable terrorism was to them:

> If the masses do not rise up spontaneously, none of this will lead to anything... For as long as we fail to treat speculators the way they deserve – with a bullet in the head – we will not get anywhere at all.[105]

One of the most important leaders of the October Revolution in Russia, Trotsky, says this to confirm Lenin's words:

> But the revolution does require of the revolutionary class that it should atta-

RUSSIAN OPPRESSION

The oppression experienced in the Russian revolution was reflected in pictures.

in its end by all methods at its disposal—**if necessary, by an armed rising: if required, by terrorism.**[106]

Trotsky went even further in another speech,

> Our only choice now is civil war. Civil war is the struggle for bread… Long live civil war![107]

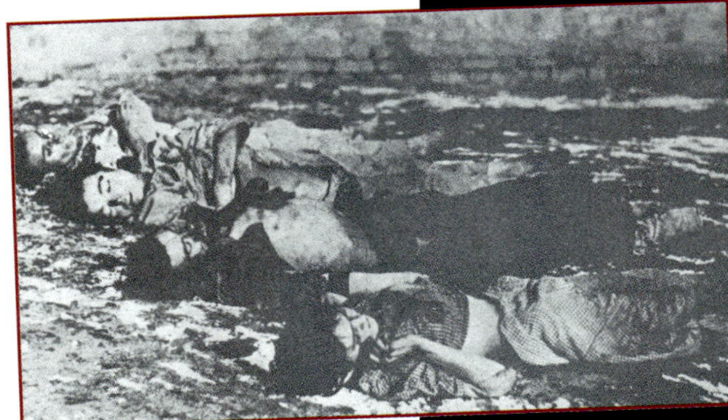

These principles of such Communist theoreticians as Lenin and Trotsky were put into practice in the Bolshevik revolution in Russia. During the revolutionary period of autumn 1917 there began wide-ranging massacres, looting, and unbelievable violence. Those people who were against the revolution, or who were suspected of being against the revolution, were rounded up for no reason, arrested, and shot: houses were looted and wrecked. Terrorism, which began with Lenin and Trotsky continued and grew worse in the Stalin years.

Harrison E. Salisbury of *The New York Times* described the Soviet system's prison camps as:

> …a whole continent of terror… Compared with those who brought about the hundreds of thousands of executions and the millions of deaths in the Soviet terror system, the Czars seem almost benign… Our minds boggle at the thought of a systematized, routine evil, under which three or four or more million men and women were sentenced each year to forced labour and eternal exile–and in a manner so casual that the prisoners often were not even told what their sentences were…[108]

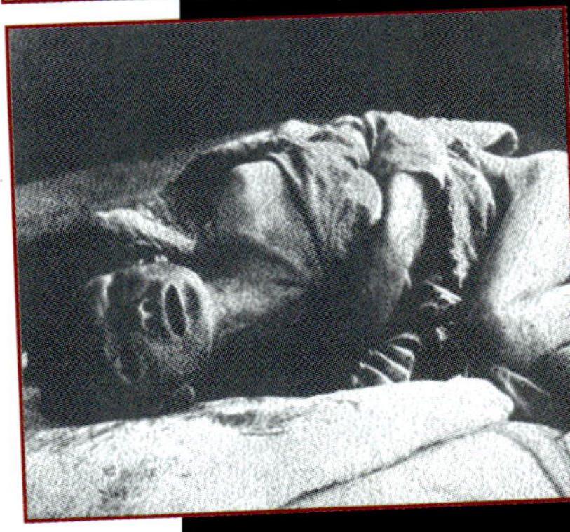

The results of the 1921-1922 famine, brought about by the Communist regime, were most painful. The pictures show people who died of starvation.

Non-Russian peoples, and particularly the Crimean Turks, the Central Asian Turks, and the Kazakhs, were exposed to the terrorism of the Soviet system. Special courts, *troiki*, were established to cleanse Russian society of the Kazakhs. In October 1920 alone these *troiki* sentenced more than 6,000 people to death, and these orders were immediately carried out. The families, and sometimes even the neighbours, of those who opposed the regime and were not apprehended, were systematically taken hostage and sent to concentration camps. Martin Latsis, the head of one of these camps in the Ukraine admitted that these were death camps in one of his reports:

The Russian government's taking villagers' produce in the Ukraine led to people dying of starvation.

What reason could you have for not fighting in the Way of Allah for those men, women, and children who are oppressed and say, 'Our Lord, take us out of this city whose inhabitants are wrongdoers! Give us a protector from You! Give us a helper from You!'?
(Surat an-Nisa: 75)

Gathered together in a camp near Maikop, the hostages, women, children, and old men survive in the most appalling conditions, in the cold and mud of October... They are dying like flies. The women will do anything to escape death. The soldiers guarding the camp take advantage of this and treat them as prostitutes.[109]

Under the influence of Darwin, the Communist revolutionaries were killing people in a crazed manner. It appears from documents of the time that the sole aim was total extermination. It was as if they believed that the more people they killed, the greater success they would have. That they planned to wipe out everybody they suspected of being against the revolution is revealed in one of their decisions:

The Pyatigorsk Cheka (Extraordinary Committee for War Against the Counter-Revolution) **decided straight out to execute 300 people a day**. They divided up the town into various boroughs and took a quota of people from each, and ordered the Party to draw up execution lists...**In Kislovodsk, for lack of a better idea, it was decided to kill people who were in the hospital**.[110]

As was announced in the lead article of the newspaper *Krasnyi Mech* (The Red Sword), which was Communist supporting, the Communists saw everything as permissible and believed that blood had to be spilt for the colour of the Red flag to come about.

To us, everything is permitted, for we are the first to raise the sword not to oppress races and reduce them to slavery, but to liberate humanity from its shackles... **Blood? Let blood flow like water! Let blood stain forever the black pirate's flag flown by the bourgeoisie, and let our flag be blood-red forever!** For only through the death of the old world can we liberate ourselves forever from the return of those jackals![111]

As well as all this torture, Stalin set up "requisitioning detachments" to take the peasants" produce by force. These units were responsible for all kinds of oppression. On 14 February 1922 one inspector wrote:

Abuses of position by the requisitioning detachments, frankly speaking, have now reached unbelievable levels. Systematically, the peasants who are arrested are all locked up in big unheated barns; they are then whipped and

"Requisioning Detachments" were set up by Stalin, and as well as torturing, they seized villagers' produce. These units oppressed the people in various ways. Those who could not find enough produce to give to the state officials were tortured to death in a number of ways.
Page across: the dreadful state of people under Communist rule.

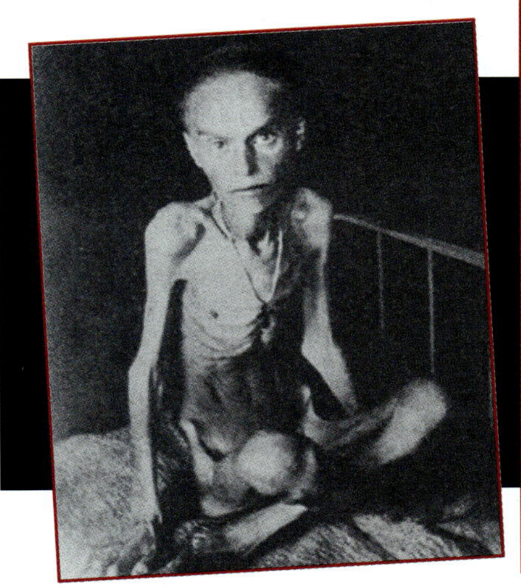

threatened with execution. Those who have not filled the whole of their quota are bound and forced to run naked all along the main street of the village and then locked up in another unheated hangar. A great number of women have been beaten until they are unconscious and then thrown naked into holes dug in the snow...[112]

Stalin believed that Spain represented opportunities for the USSR and that meddling in that country would bear fruit. For that reason he took sides and supported the Communists in the Spanish Civil War. But with that the terrorism in the USSR overflowed into Spain. One example of the oppression and torture there was the concentration camp that 200 anti-Stalinists were held in at the beginning of 1938. "When the Stalinists decided to open a cheka," one victim recalled;

> There was a small cemetery being cleaned out nearby. The Chekists had a diabolical idea: they would leave the cemetery's tombs open, with the skeletons and the decomposing bodies in full view. That's where they locked up the most difficult cases. They had some particularly brutal methods of torture. Many prisoners were hung up by their feet, upside down, for whole days. Others they locked in tiny cupboards with just a tiny air hole near the face to breathe through... One of the worst methods was known as "the drawer"; prisoners were forced to squat in tiny square boxes for several days. Some were kept there unable to move for eight to ten days.[113]

In 1931 Pope Pius XI had this to say about the violence Communism had inflicted on the world in the encyclical *Quadragesimo Anno*:

Communism teaches and seeks two objectives: **unrelenting class warfare and the complete eradication of private ownership**. Not secretly or by hidden methods does it do this, but publicly, openly, and by employing any means possible, even the most violent. To achieve these objectives there is nothing it is afraid to do, nothing for which it has respect or reverence. When comes to power, it is ferocious in its cruelty and inhumanity. **The horrible slaughter and destruction through which it has laid waste vast regions of Eastern Europe and Asia give evidence of this.**[114]

As the above extract says, Communism's principle aims were a merciless class war and the complete doing away with private property. In other words the aim was to apply the theory of evolution, which Darwin had applied in the biological field, to human societies, and for human beings to be, like wild animals in nature, in conflict, at war.

The disasters brought about by Communism did not stop in Russia. One of the countries worst affected among those to which it spread was China.

The Darwinist Mao Tse-Tung and His Massacres

China's Communist leader Mao had two important guides: one of these, as we touched on earlier, was Darwin, and the other was Stalin. These two lethal names, which met together in Mao's personality, led to great tragedies and left their mark on a long, dark period in Chinese history. Between 6 to 10 million people were directly killed under Mao Tse-Tung's directives, tens of millions of counter-revolutionaries spent great parts of their lives in prison, where 20 million of them died. Between 20 and 40 million people died of starvation in the years 1959-1961, in the period called "The Great Leap Forward," as the dreadful result of Mao's extremist policies. The June 1989 Tienanmen Square massacre (about 1,000 dead) is one example of what China has gone through in its recent history. The killings and genocide directed against the Muslim Turks in Eastern Turkestan are still going on.

Great savagery and unbelievable things took place when the Communist revolution happened in China. The people, who were under the

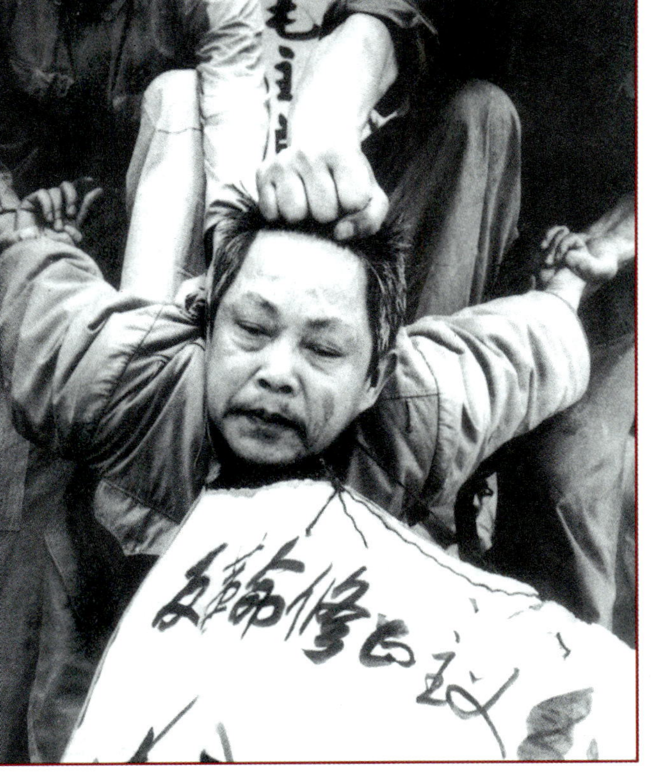

effects of a kind of mass hypnotism, supported all kinds of savagery and showed that support by shouting as they watched the killings. The book *Le Livre Noir du Communisme* ("The Black Book of Communism"), prepared by a group of historians and teachers, described Communism's savage practices in this way:

The whole people were invited to public trials of "counter-revolutionaries," who almost invariably were condemned to death. Everyone participated in the executions, shouting out "kill, kill" to the Red Guards whose task it was to cut victims into pieces. Sometimes the pieces were cooked and eaten, or force-fed to members of the victim's family who were still alive and looking on. Everyone was then invited to a banquet, where the liver and heart of the former landowner were shared out, and to meetings where the speaker would address rows of severed heads freshly skewered on stakes. This fascination for vengeful cannibalism, which later became common under the Pol Pot regime, echoes a very ancient East Asian archetype that appears often at cataclysmic moments of Chinese history.[115]

Communist supporters of Mao punished those who opposed them in the civil war in ruthless ways, humiliating them in front of the people and then executing them.

Chinese party leaders accused of being capitalists first had their heads shaved in front of the people and were then executed.

The execution of a Chinese woman, Wang Souxin. The money for the bullets used in executions in Red China was extracted from the relatives of the victims.

POL POT AND THE KHMER ROUGE "KILLING FIELDS"

Between 1975 and 1979, during the rule of Pol Pot, two million of Cambodia's population of seven million were killed. When one looks at the killings by Pol Pot, who dreamed of establishing a perfect Communist state, as a percentage of the population, then his killings were much greater than those by Hitler and Stalin. Pol Pot's fundamental target were the sections of society such as doctors, engineers, scientists, in short the country's intellectuals, whom he had killed. The order was even given that "everyone wearing glasses" should be killed. As a result of these inhuman murders, the "killing fields," which lasted for years, emerged.

The logic employed by the Khmer Rouge officers to justify their massacres was summed up in these words: "Keeping you is no gain. Losing you is no loss" They killed everyone whom they considered to be, or even suspected of being, useless or harmful. At least one member of every family lost his life in these massacres.

Pol Pot, who counted human life as nothing, believed that the family stood in the way of his radical vision of socialism. He tried to do away with the idea of the family by splitting families up and obliging human beings to live in communal places. The same policy had been implemented by Stalin in Russia. First the peasants' lands were taken from them, then small parcels of land given back, in areas deliberately scattered and far removed from one another. The result of this was that in order for a family to work their fields which consisted of tiny parcels of land they would have to live separate from one another.

Robert Templer, *Pol Pot's Legacy of Horror*, The Age, April 18, 1998, http://dithpran.org/PolPotegacy.htm

Pol Pot and the Khmer Rouge turned the country into "Killing Fields."

The Bitter Toll of Communist Savagery

Similar examples of savagery were experienced in every country Communism took over, Cambodia, North Korea, Laos, Vietnam and Eastern European and African countries. This bloody toll is set out in *The Black Book of Communism* as follows:

These crimes tend to fit a recognizable pattern even if the practices vary to some extent by regime. The pattern includes execution by various means, such as firing squads, hanging, drowning, battering, and, in certain cases, gassing, poisoning, or "car accidents"; destruction of the population by starvation, through man-made famine, the withholding of food, or both; deportation, through which death can occur in transit (either through physical exhaustion or through confinement in an enclosed space), at one's place of residence, or through forced labour (exhaustion, illness, hunger, cold). Periods described as times of "civil war" are more complex – it is not always easy to distinguish between events caused by fighting between rulers and rebels and events that can properly be described only as a massacre of the civilian population.

Noneless, we have to start somewhere. The following rough approximation, based on unofficial estimates, gives some sense of the scale and gravity of these crimes:

U.S.S.R.: 20 million deaths

China: 65 million deaths

Vietnam: 1 million deaths

North Korea: 2 million deaths

Cambodia: 2 million deaths

Eastern Europe: 1 million deaths

Latin America: 150,000 deaths

Africa: 1.7 million deaths

Afghanistan: 1.5 million deaths

The international Communist movement and Communist parties not in power: about 10,000 deaths

The total approaches 100 million people killed.[116]

All these different Communist regimes and organisations shared one common psychology: all human feelings such as pity, justice, and compassion had been completely lost. All of a sudden human societies had become fields of war and massacre wild animals tried to live and find food. In the same way as a wild animal fights with other members of its own species over food and territory, so these people behaved like "animals" in the same way. Because the birth of Darwin had taught them that they were basically animals, and as animals fight for survival, so they would have to behave in the same way.

These inhuman movements thought that they had won respectability by wearing a false scientific mask. The only reason the Bolshevik leaders were able to talk so boldly and openly of aggression, terrorism, and massacre was the approval they got from Darwin's theory of evolution. In his book *Evolution for Naturalists*, P. J. Darlington admits, as an evolutionist, that savagery is a natural result of the theory of evolution and that this behaviour is even justified:

> The first point is that selfishness and violent are inherent in us, inherited from our remotest animal ancestors... **Violence is, then, natural to man, a product of evolution.**[117]

As is clear from this evolutionist's admission, it was perfectly natural for Communist ideology, which accepted Darwin's theory of evolution as its guide, to perceive other human beings as animals, treat them in a manner befitting animals, and oppress them. Because he who accepts Communist-Darwinist ideology forgets that he has a Creator, the reason for his being in the world, and that he will have to give an account of what he has done to Him on the Day of Judgement. And as a result of this, like every human being who has no fear of Allah, he comes to be a selfish thing who thinks only of his own interests, a pitiless tyrant, even a wild-eyed killer. Allah reveals these peoples' situation and what will happen to them in this way:

> **There are only grounds against those who wrong people and act as tyrants in the earth without any right to do so. Such people will have a painful punishment. (Surat ash-Shura: 42)**

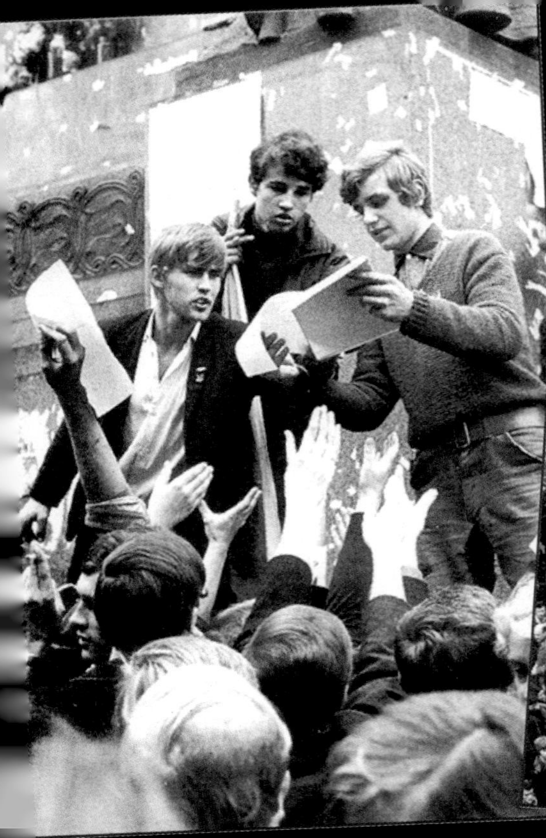

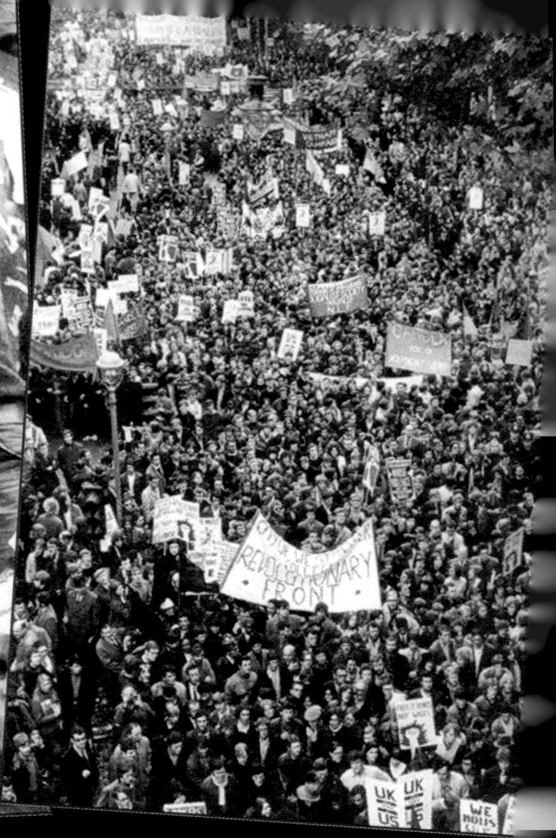

REVOLUTIONARY
FRONT
UK
US
WE
NOUS

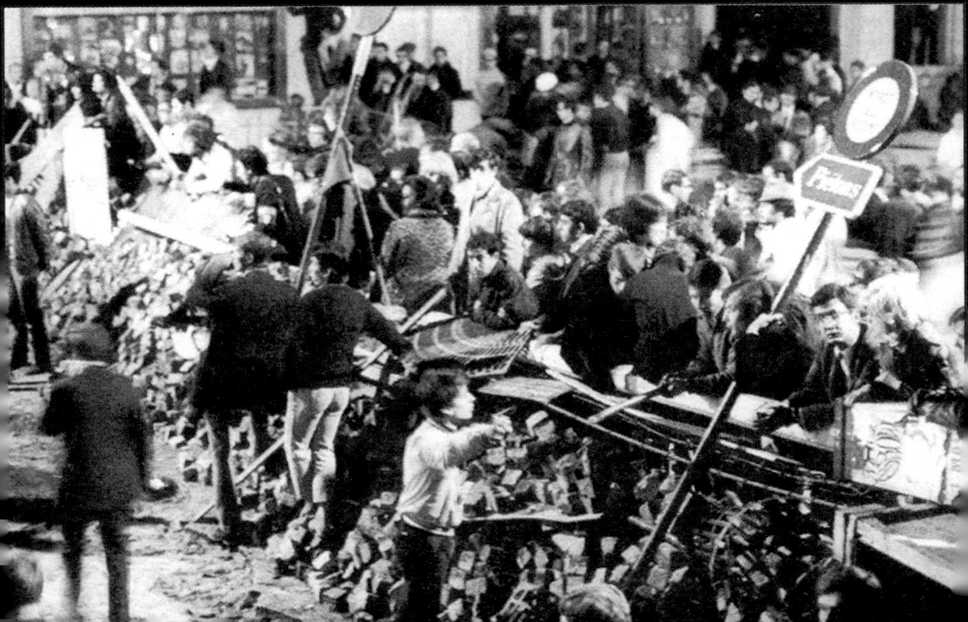

In 1968 left-wing ideology affected all parts of the world, particularly young people in universities. Meetings were held, and young people were incited against their own compatriots, the police, and the military. By virtue of these events, where brother attacked brother, cities were devastated, and the whole world fell into chaos.

THE OPPRESSION IN EASTERN TURKESTAN

No matter how much it is accepted that the dissolution of the Soviet Union spelt the end of Communism as a political regime, Communist ideology and practice still continue. The practices of Russia, where the Red Army mentality still dominates, in Chechnya, and of China in Eastern Turkestan, are the most important indications of this. The Muslim Turks who live today in Eastern Turkestan, are going through a repetition of the experiences of Mao's Red China. Young people are arrested for no reason, sentenced to death on the grounds they are opponents of the regime, and shot, Muslims are prevented from carrying out their group religious duties, their earnings are taken from them by means of ruthless taxes, the people live on the edge of death through the threat of starvation, and the nuclear tests carried out right next to them cause them to catch fatal diseases.

The Muslim Turks of Eastern Turkestan have been living under Chinese hegemony for 250 years. The Chinese gave the name "Sinkiang" or "conquered lands" to Eastern Turkestan, a Muslim land, and defined it as their own territory. After the Communists led by Mao took it over in 1949, the pressure on Eastern Turkestan increased to even higher levels than before. The policy of the Communist regime aimed at the physical destruction of the Muslims, who rejected assimilation. The number of Muslims killed reached terrifying proportions. Between 1949 and 1952, 2,800,000; between 1952 and 1957, 3,509,000; between 1958 and 1960, 6,700,000; between 1961 and 1965, 13,300,000 people were either killed by the Chinese Army or died as a result of the shortages brought about by the regime. Together with the massacres after 1965, the number of Eastern Turkestan people killed reached the unbelievable figure of 35 million.

As well as wiping out the Muslims since 1949, the regime also systematically moved Chinese settlers in. The effects of this campaign, which the Chinese government began in 1953, are most thought-provoking. While in 1953, 75% of the population was Muslim and 6% Chinese, by 1982 the figures were 43% Muslim and 40% Chinese. The 1990 census, which revealed that the population figures were now 40% Muslim and 53% Chinese, is most important from the point of view of revealing the scale of the ethnic cleansing.

Meanwhile, the Chinese administration used the Eastern Turkestan Muslims as experimental animals in their nuclear tests. As a result of the nuclear tests, which first started in the region in 1964, local people have been infected by deadly diseases, and 20,000 handicapped children have been born. It is known that the number of Muslims who have died because of the tests is 210,000. Thousands of people have been crippled, and thousands have fallen prey to such diseases as jaundice and cancer.

Between 1964 and the present, China has exploded some 50 atomic and hydrogen bombs. Swedish experts established that an underground nuclear test in 1984 of a bomb with a force of 150 tons had resulted in earth tremors of a magnitude of 8.8 on the Richter scale.

China's oppression of the Uighur Turks does not stop there. The experiences of February, 1997, during a time when incidents were increasingly flaring up, will serve to sum up the Chinese oppression. According to news reported to the public, on Sept. 4, which happened to be a feast day, Chinese militia forces beat more than 30 women, who had gathered in a mosque and were reading out from the Qur'an, with iron bars and dragged them to security headquarters. The local residents went to the head-quarters and asked for the women to be released. At that point the bodies of three women who had been tortured to death were thrown in front of them. Then clashes began between the people, who rose to the provocation, and the Chinese. Between Sept. 4 and 7, 200 Eastern Turkestan people lost their lives and more than 3,500 Uighur Turks were locked up in camps. On the morning of Sept. 8, people were prevented by the security forces from offering holiday prayers in the mosques where they had gathered. Following this the clashes flared up again, and as a result the number of detained, which had been 58,000 between April and December 1996, went past 70,000. As many as 100 young people were shot in public squares, and 5,000 Uighur Turks were stripped naked and publicly exhibited in groups of 50.

The example of Eastern Turkestan is just one of the sufferings in the 20th century. In every corner of the world in the 20th century people of different religions, races, or ideologies killed and exterminated each other. It is no coincidence that behind all the ideologies which did these killings Darwin's world view should emerge. Because with his theory Darwin made it easy for people to kill each other and justify their actions.

When those who did wrong see the punishment, it will not be lightened for them. They will be granted no reprieve. (Surat an-Naml: 85)

However, those who do wrong pursue their whims and desires without any knowledge. Who can guide those whom Allah has led astray? They will have no helpers. (Surat ar-Rum: 29)

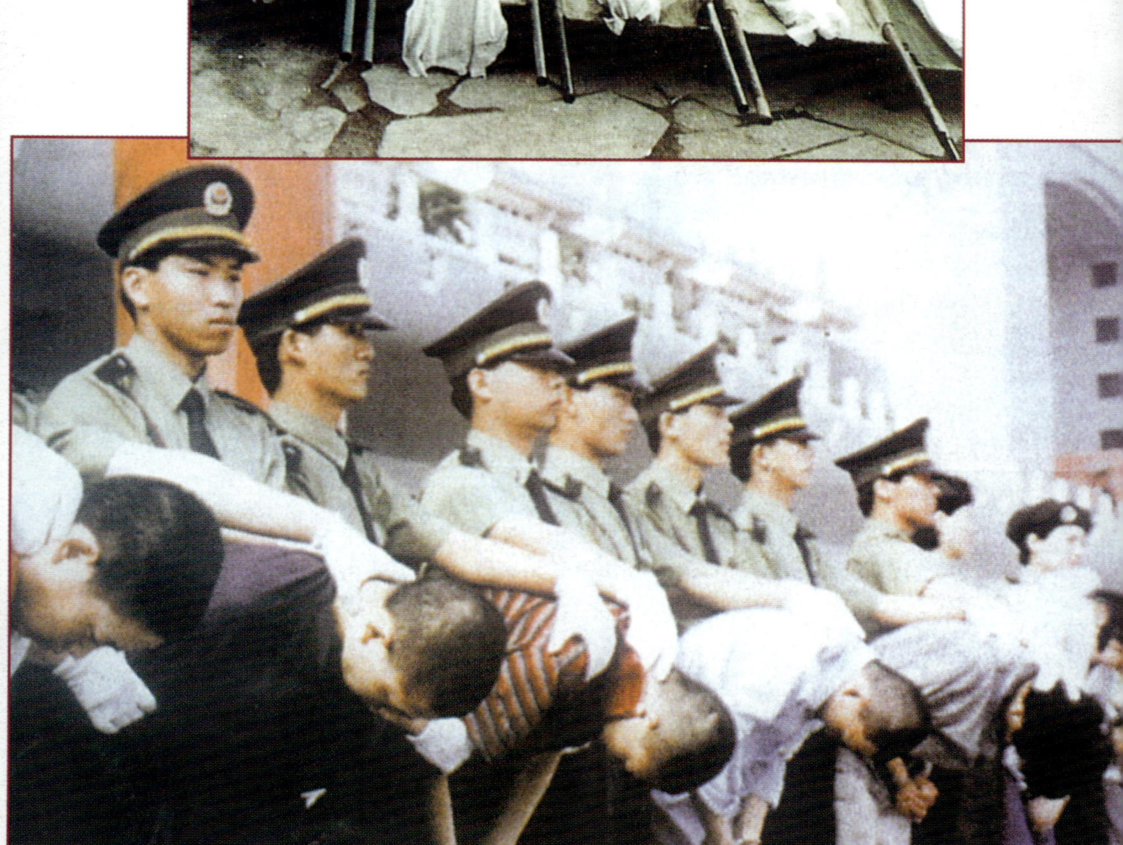

Those to whom people said,
"The people have gathered against
you, so fear them." But that merely
increased their faith and they said,
"Allah is enough for us. He is the Best
of Guardians." (Surah Al 'Imran: 173)

AMNESTY INTERNATIONAL BRIEFING
CHINA:
No one is safe
abuse of power
torture
executions
amnesty international briefing

THE NEVER-ENDING OPPRESSION IN CHECHNYA

The Russian occupation of Chechnya in 1991, despite being thrown back by the late Dzhokar Dudayev, turned into a genuine war on Dec. 11, 1994, following serious trouble in November that same year. While more than 100,000 Chechens lost their lives in that war, tens of thousands were forced to migrate. Chechnya lost hundreds of historical and economic resources in the war. When Russia announced that Chechnya was an "internal matter," no protest came from the outside world. Tons of bombs fell on every square metre in Chechnya. A genocide was carried out, the like of which has never been seen in the history of the world, with chemical weapons, the use of which was forbidden ant it still continues today. But despite all the difficulties, in August 1996 the Russians had to admit defeat at the hands of the Chechens, who were completely undaunted and fought for their own land with all the means at their disposal.

Russia, which had to accept Chechnya as a separate state in agreements signed at the highest levels in August 1996 and May 1997, seemed to have accepted this situation. Whereas in October

1997 the Russians entered Chechen territory and began to kill, not sparing women, children, and the elderly. Civilian targets came under non-stop bombardment for months. In order to break the popular resistance, hospitals, maternity wards, markets, and refugee convoys were especially chosen as targets. At the last it was established that the Russians used chemical bombs and scud and napalm missiles against the Chechens. Alongside this, the Russians put poison into the River Argun, used by many Chechen villages. While the great majority of the women and children who drank the poisoned water died, hundreds waited for death at the doors of the hospitals. Because the river water had been poisoned the civilian population who were unable to find water for drinking and other purposes went through very difficult times.

The situation of the refugees was also worrying. Studies carried out in refugee areas showed that human rights infringements reached enormous proportions. Some 250,000 Chechen refugees who fled from the war are under protection in Ingushetya, the rest in neighbouring regions. It has been announced that Russia spent 385 million dollars on the operation. The Chechens revealed that between September 1999 and July 25, 2000, 1,460 Chechen soldiers and 45,000 civilians had died. Russia's plan was to wipe out all the Chechen soldiers who had been fighting them by November 2000.

Newsweek 13 February 1995

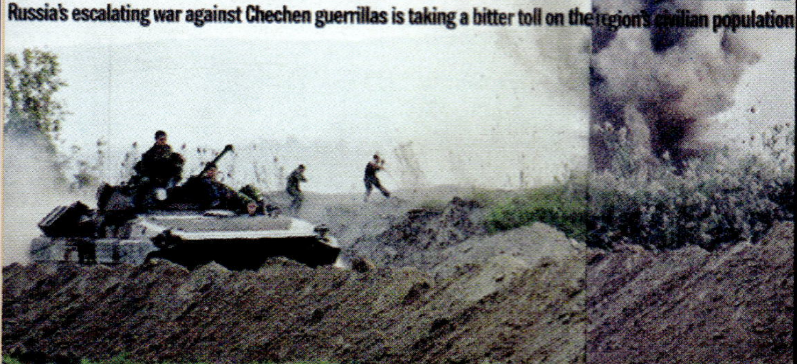

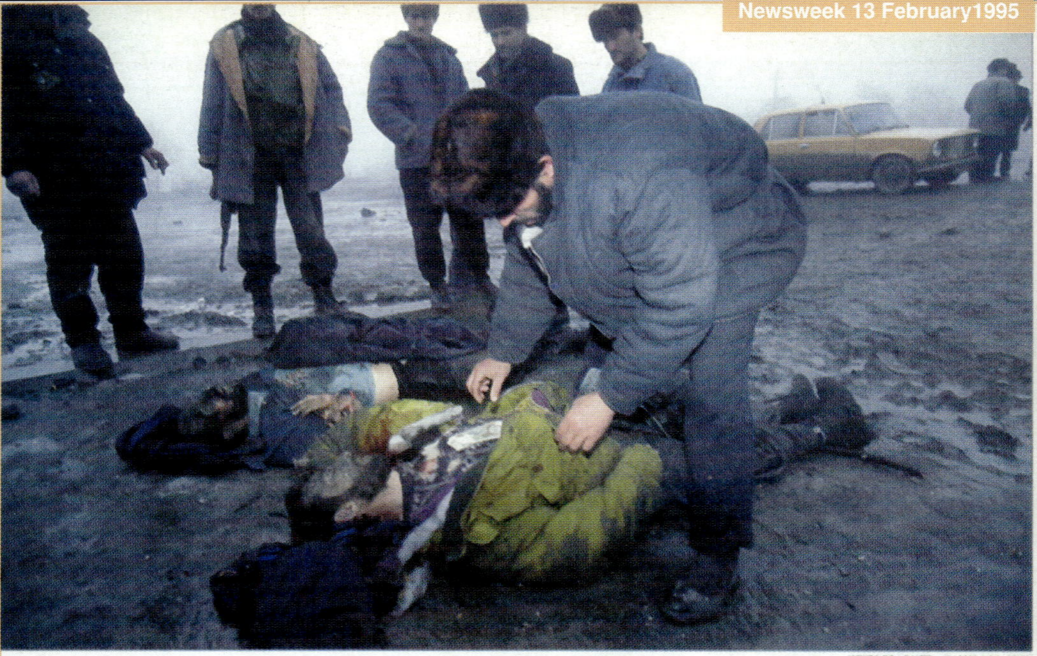

HEIDI BRADNER—GAMMA-LIAISON

'Disproportionate': *Victims of a Russian bombing raid on a civilian market near Grozny, the Chechen capital*

Dire Tales of a Dirty War

Chechnya: Locals accuse the Russians of atrocities

"WE HAVE ENOUGH INFORMATION TO detain you." The offhanded com-

dok, the Russians' rear base for Chechnya, hundreds of Chechens and even some local

in Chechnya" as one of the year's black moments. President Bill Clinton has repeatedly warned Yeltsin in phone conversations: although the United States recognizes Russia's territorial claim to Chechnya, Yeltsin should appreciate how Russia's tactics are hurting its international standing. Are the Russians getting the message? "There doesn't seem to be much evidence of that," says a senior U.S. official

Newsweek 1 November 1999

E U R O P E

THE FATAL FRONTIER

Russia's escalating war against Chechen guerrillas is taking a bitter toll on the region's civilian population

By PAUL QUINN-JUDGE MOSCOW

IT WAS A SCENE THAT IS BECOMING ALL too common in the new wars of Eastern Europe: by the time the smoke had cleared on Thursday in central Grozny some 60 bleeding, mangled bodies lay sprawled in the blasted remains of an open-air market, with hundreds more wounded. The cause, Chechens claimed, was one or more Scuds—a medium-range missile capable of inflicting massive damage on troops or equipment—fired into the capital of the

crossed the River Terek, 20 km northeast of the capital, and had started to fight their way toward Grozny in the second phase of this latest Chechen war. The first phase had been a largely triumphal procession through the sparsely populated northern plains, but the real war is for the towns and villages of the rugged south where Chechen rebels humiliated the Russian army in 1994-96. Its bloodiness could soon eclipse the rocket attack.

The push on the south started late last week when Russian troops reportedly crossed the Terek on pontoons and rafts.

the military seemed eager to move. "Grozny and other population centers will be liberated from terrorists," General Valery Manilov announced, and Russian military officials said they expect an attack on the city toward the end of this week.

Whether or not the missile attack on Grozny was a mistake, it fitted neatly into a Moscow strategy cynically intended to create refugees. Russian officials have made no secret of the fact that they want as many civilians as possible out of Grozny before they send their troops in. That pattern was followed in attacks in other parts of Chech-

Russian air and artillery attacks, or the fear of them, have sent some 184,000 people—about 45% of Chechnya's population—fleeing into neighboring areas. But there will still be plenty of civilians left when the battle for the city comes. The old, the sick and the poor will remain. Ironically, many of them will be ethnic Russians with nowhere to go and no relatives in the countryside to give them shelter.

Though less than a month old, the war has already exacted a terrible toll on civilians. There are no accurate figures on noncombatant casualties, but estimates begin

time the ratio of civilian deaths will be higher, Basaev predicted in a recent interview, because the Chechen resistance is better prepared and more experienced.

The prospect of civilian carnage will not deter the military of either side. In the days leading up to the crossing of the Terek, bombastic declarations from Moscow and Grozny made one thing painfully clear: Chechen and Russian commanders are raring for war. On the Russian side, the generals who presided over the murderous debacle of 1994-96 want revenge. In Chechnya, hard-liners like Shamil Basayev, a top field

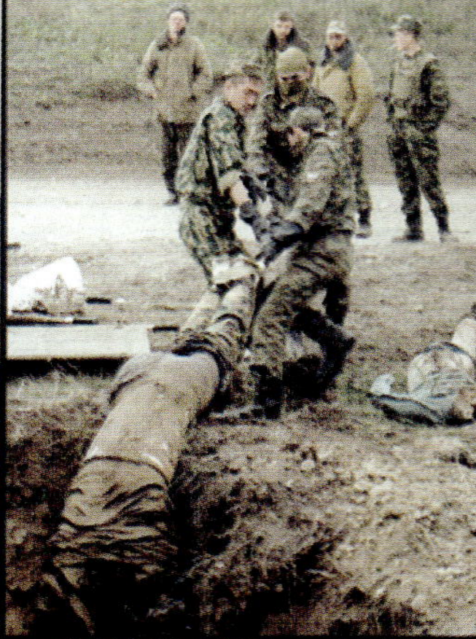

BATTLE READY: The total war that both Chechen and Russian military leaders [illegible] they crave may already be under way

destined by ominous statements with [illegible] ly identical sentiments from Moscow [illegible] Grozny. Both say they want to fight to [illegible] death. "When the last bandit is destroy[illegible] our task will be completed," said L[illegible] General Gennady Troshin, a Russian [illegible] mander. He seemed to have been bor[illegible] ing lines from the Chechens. Kavkaz[illegible] ter, an Internet-based news service clo[illegible] Basayev, reported that the Chechen [illegible] Defense Committee was discussing a

CHECHEN HELL

On the front lines of Russia's brutal battle for control of the Caucasus

By PAUL QUINN-JUDGE GUDERMES

GENERAL ALEXA... MIKHAILOV clearly wishes ... where else. "I ... ing these mo... ago," he com... wait in Mozd... three hours by plane ... the nerve center of ... Chechnya. There is ...

Salman Raduyev had seized the village, taken hostages and for days beaten back attacks by élite Russian units. Mikhailov was ...ponsible for explaining this mortifying ... to the world. His ... as ...

shot. Now, as Russian guns, warplanes and missiles reduce to rubble what was left of Gudermes after the 1994-96 war, Russian officials talk increasingly of turning this grim railway town with a peacetime population of 38,000 into Chechnya's new capital... problem, says a Russian airborne ... forward base jus...

Morning After the Terror

A razed village mourns the victims of Moscow's missiles. A rebel leader escapes to fight again

By MICHAEL S. SERRILL

THE SMALL RUSSIAN VILLAGE OF Pervomaiskoye was in ruins last week. The terror had swirled around it, flattened it like some crazed tornado and now was ebbing. The once scarcely known town began resuming its anonymity. But while the world will soon forget the disaster there, dazed villagers faced years of trying to reassemble what little they had.

After many harrowing days, for a few others there was a happy ending. In Chechnya last week, rebel guerrillas put 46 civilian hostages aboard a bus and let them return home to the neighboring Russian region of Dagestan. Two weeks before, more than 100 Chechen guerrillas seized 3,000 hostages in Dagestan, then were trapped in Pervomaiskoye and bombarded mercilessly. After the barrage ended, it became embarrassingly clear that dozens of rebels had slipped through the lines. Among them: the rebel leader, Salman Raduyev. Most of the original hostages had been freed during the crisis, but an unknown number were killed, as were some 50 rebels. Villagers returning to Pervomaiskoye were overwhelmed. "I was surprised by their lack of emotion," says photographer Jason Eskenazi, who captured the devastation on film for TIME. "They did not seem to be stunned by what had happened to their village, but just resigned."

VILLAGE OF THE DAMNED: Some of the 870 residents of the ravaged town of Pervomaiskoye began drifting back to their homes last week. But they found only dead bodies and devastation. Russia says it will rebuild

THE SPELL OF COMMUNIST DARWINIST IDEOLOGY IS DISPERSED

Communism is an ideology which was brought into being by people who lived in the 1800s, and who can be described as "ignorant" from the scientific point of view. One of the most important reasons for the rapid winning of influence over wide sections of the peoples of many country's by this ideology, whose analysis and claims have been proven false many times and which furthermore has clearly brought harm to mankind and not good, is the ignorance of those human beings who accepted this ideology.

After the Industrial Revolution, one part of society's being in terrible poverty, and alongside this, another part's rising to an incomparable level of well being, brought out a tension open to agitation in social groups in most countries. This tension developed in countries such as Russia, still living on the level of an agricultural society, and China. Social groups looking for right and justice followed along behind. But the end result worked against them. They lived under far worse economic conditions than before, on the one hand struggling to avoid dying of hunger, on the other living with the fear and terror of being killed at any moment, torture, exile, and robbery.

It was evident that that an ideology based on lack of religion, which believed that the sole basis for development was conflict, fighting, and war, that human beings are basically animals, based on the deviation that moral values such as family, faithfulness, and closeness are unnecessary and irrelevant, would not bring people peace, security, happiness, and justice. But these social groups lacked the vision and understanding to evaluate and analyse these. They looked at photographs of Marx and Engels and thought them to be most "deep," "incomprehensible," and "knowledgeable" thinkers. They looked at the illusory scientific and deep exteri-

or and the syrupy manners of those who supported them and fell under the spell of Communism and materialism. Whereas today, had they been alive, they would have understood that every Communist leader had a very coarse and primitive understanding and were ignorant people.

None of the people they accepted as leaders behaved in a forward-looking manner, they were only able to bind social groups to them by insults and fear: they were people who adopted violence, savagery, ruthlessness, and murder as methods, and thought in a coarse and primitive way. Today many an "old time" Communist has realised what a great mistake he made in the past and regretted it. Each one has understood that he had blindly followed an unproductive ideal, or rather an empty, loud noise. Others try to show that they have still not given their ideology up in order not to accept the defeat and the truth that the years were wasted and say, "We shall overcome."

A period has begun when science and free knowledge can reach anywhere at any time, when any human being can realise truths and realities much easier than before, and to a greater degree. In such an environment the methods of suggestion, reminiscent of a magic spell, of the Communists, materialists, and Darwinists, their talismanic words and calls to war have now lost their power. Hollow ideologies such as Communism, materialism, and Darwinism, whose spellbinding power can be lifted with a little science and a little thought, are rapidly losing their influence on human beings. As a result of this, lighter, more peaceful and comfortable days await mankind. Most important, the realisation of the deception of Darwinism, with full proof, will bring about the end of these ideologies.

Conclusion: Communism is a Terror Brought About by Lack of Religion

Anyone who considers the massacres, murders, and the suffering deliberately inflicted on human beings by the Communists, Nazis, or colonialists, will wonder how the supporters of these ideas could have distanced themselves so far from common humanity. The sole reason for the savagery and oppression inflicted by these leaders is lack of religion and the fact these people had no fear of God. A human being who fears God and who has firm faith in the hereafter, will definitely be incapable of carrying out any of the oppression, wrongs, injustice, and murders that we have described. Furthermore, no matter how much he may be encouraged, someone who believes in God and the hereafter will never be pulled into following such a deviant ideology.

But people who have no religion and no fear of God know no limits. With a bit of encouragement a person who believes that he and other living creatures evolved by coincidence out of non-living matter, who believes that his ancestors were animals, and who accepts that nothing exists apart from the material, can easily carry out any kind of cruelty. At first sight perhaps these people might seem as if they do not hurt anybody: but given the right circumstances they can turn into a killer who carries out massacres, assassins who beat people or starve them just because they do not accept their ideas, people filled with hatred, loathing, and violence. Because the world view and values they believe in necessitate this.

In 1983, Alexander I. Solzhenitsyn, winner of the 1970 Nobel-prize for literature, gave an address in London in which he attempted to explain why so much evil had befallen his people:

> Over a half century ago, while I was still a child, I recall hearing a number of old people offer the following explanation for the great disasters that had befallen Russia: **"Men have forgotten God; that's why all this has happened."**
>
> Since then I have spend well-nigh 50 years working on the history of our revolution; in the process I have read hundreds of books, collected hundreds

of personal testimonies, and have already contributed eight volumes of my own toward the effort of clearing away the rubble left by that upheaval. But if I were asked today to formulate as concisely as possible the main cause of the ruinous revolution that swallowed up some 60 million of our people, I could not put it more accurately than to repeat: **"Men have forgotten God; that's why all this has happened."**[118]

This identification of Solzhenitsyn's was utterly accurate. Really, the only thing that could drag a society into that much terror, to turn a blind eye to all kinds of oppression, to watch from the sidelines, is the forgetting of God. Whereas God never forgets and is never mistaken. The ruthless Communist leaders thought that they had set up their own system to rule societies on earth and thought that they possessed a great power and strength. They even held secret meetings, where they whispered to each other of the further oppression they would inflict on people to increase their power and strength. But while they were doing all this, God knew of it, and He will answer what they have done. He announces it in the Qur'an:

> **On the Day Allah raises up all of them together, He will inform them of what they did. Allah has recorded it while they have forgotten it. Allah is a Witness of all things. Do you not see that Allah knows what is in the heavens and on the earth? Three men cannot confer together secretly without Him being the fourth of them, or five without Him being the sixth of them, or fewer than that or more without Him being with them wherever they are. Then He will inform them on the Day of Rising of what they did. Allah has knowledge of all things. (Surat al-Mujadila: 6-7)**

Then there are the groups who followed these ruthless leaders, who crawled along behind them. Their situation has been revealed in the Qur'an. It was announced in the verse **"Allah does not wrong people in any way; rather it is people who wrong themselves." (Surah Yunus: 44)** In other words these people oppressed themselves by forgetting the religion of Allah and following Darwinist leaders. Another holy verse announces that people bring about the evil that happens in the world themselves:

Corruption has appeared in both land and sea because of what people's own hands have brought about so that they may taste something of what they have done so that hopefully they will turn back. (Surat ar-Rum: 41)

The only way to prevent these disasters from bringing harm to mankind again is for people to live with faith in Allah and the hereafter and without forgetting that they will have to account for everything they do. And, in the light of the Qur'an, which Allah sent down for all people, for them to possess the good moral features, such as love, compassion, mercy, and devotion, which are commanded in it.

Anyone who acts rightly, male or female, being a believer, We will give them a good life and We will recompense them according to the best of what they did. (Surat an-Nahl: 97)

WRONGED PEOPLE

These pictures sum up a part of the nightmare which Communist ideology inflicted on mankind. People weakened by hunger, thirst, and hopelessness, living in poverty and need...

A regime with Darwinist-Communist views holds its people of no value. It abandons them to death and poverty with open eyes. Russia is an obvious example of this.

PART 5

CAPITALISM AND THE FIGHT FOR SURVIVAL IN THE ECONOMY

The term capitalism means the sovereignty of capital, a free and unrestricted economic system totally based on profit and where society is in competition within these criteria. There are three important elements in capitalism: individualism, competition, and profit-making. Individualism is important in capitalism, because people see themselves not as a part of society, but as "individuals" standing alone on their own two feet who have to get by with their own efforts. "Capitalist society" is an arena where individuals compete with one another under very harsh and ruthless conditions. This is an arena just like that described by Darwin, where only the strong survive, where the weak and powerless are crushed and eliminated, and where ruthless competition holds sway.

According to the logic capitalism is based on, every individual–and this can be a person, a company, or a nation–must only fight for its own development and advantage. The most important criterion in this war is production. The best producers survive, the weak and incompetent are eliminated and vanish. This being the shape of the system, it is forgotten that those who are eliminated in the bitter struggle, those who are crushed and fall into poverty, are "people." What is seen as worthy of attention is not human beings, but economic development, and goods, the product of this development. For which reason the capitalist mentality feels no ethical responsibility or conscience for the person whom it crushes underfoot and climbs on top of and who has to live in great difficulty. This is Darwinism put into total practice in society in an economic way.

By proposing that it was necessary to encourage competition in all areas of society, and announcing that it was necessary to provide no opportunities or support for the weak in any field, from health to the economy, the foremost theoreticians of Social Darwinism prepared a "philosophical" and "scientific" support for capitalism. For example, according to Tille, a foremost representative of the Darwinist-capitalist mentality, it was a great error to try to prevent poverty by helping the "defeated classes," because that meant interfering with natural selection which brought about evolution.[119]

In the view of Herbert Spencer, the main theorist of Social Darwinism, who introduced the principles of Darwinism to the life of society, if someone is poor then that is his mistake; nobody must help this person to rise. If someone is rich, even if he has acquired his wealth by immoral means, that is his competence. For this reason, the rich man survives, while the poor man disappears. This is the view which has come to prevail almost completely in today's societies and is a summary of Darwinist-capitalist morality.

Herbert Spencer

Spencer, who defended this morality, finished his work *Social Statistics* in 1850, and opposed all systems of help offered by the state, precautions for the protection of health, state schools, and compulsory inoculation. Because according to Social Darwinism, social order arose from the principle of the survival of the strong. Supporting the weak and allowing them to survive was a breach of this principle. The rich are rich because they are better fitted; some nations rule others, because they are superior to them, some races fall under the yoke of others, because these others are more intelligent than them. Spencer applied the doctrine to human societies with a vengeance: "If they are sufficiently complete to live, they do live, and it is well they should live. If they are not sufficiently complete to live, they die, and it is best they should die."[120]

Graham Sumner, Professor of Political and Social Sciences at Yale University, was Social Darwinism's spokesman in America. In one of his writings he summed up his thoughts on human societies in these words:

> …if we lift any man up we must have a fulcrum, a point of reaction. **In society that means that to lift one man up we push another down.**[121]

Richard Milner, senior editor of New York's American Museum of Natural History's *Natural History Magazine* writes:

> One of Social Darwinism's leading spokesmen, William Graham Sumner of Princeton, thought millionaires were the 'fittest' individuals in society and deserved their privileges. They were "naturally selected in the crucible of competition."[122]

As has been seen from these announcements, Social Darwinists used Darwin's theory of evolution as a "scientific" comment on capitalist societies. As a result of this, human beings began to lose such concepts, which religion had brought with it, as mutual assistance, philanthropy, and co-operation, and instead of these virtues to give pride of place to selfishness, cunning, and opportunism. According to one of Social Darwinism's most important theorists, the American Professor E. A. Ross, "The Christian cult of charity as a means of grace has formed a shelter under which idiots and cretins have crept and bred.". Again in Ross' view, "The state gathers the deaf mutes into its sheltering arm, and a race of deaf mutes is in process of formation." Rejecting all these because they prevent natural evolutionary progress, Ross declared that "The shortest way to make this world a heaven is to let those so inclined hurry hell-ward at their own pace."[123]

As we have seen, Darwinism forms the philosophical basis of all the capitalist economic systems in the world and the political systems which take their shape from them.

It is for this reason that the greatest supporters of Social Darwinism were owners of capital. The rise of the strong by treading on the weak and the following of economic policies far removed from feelings of pity, help, and compassion were no longer to be condemned, because behaviour like this was accepted as in accordance with "scientific explanations" and "the laws of nature."

According to Richard Hofstadter, the author of the book *Social Darwinism in American Thought*, the nineteenth-century railroad magnate Chauncey Depew asserted that the men who attained fame, fortune, and power in New York City represented the survival of the fittest, through "superior ability, foresight and adaptability."[124] Another railroad baron, James

J. Hill, alleged that "the fortunes of railroad companies are determined by the law of the survival of the fittest."[125]

In his biography Andrew Carnegie, another major owner of capital in America, states his belief in evolution with the words, "I had found the truth of evolution."[126] Elsewhere he wrote these words:

> **It (the law of competition) is here**; we cannot evade it; no substitutes for it have been found; and while the law may sometimes be hard for the individual, it is best for the race, because **it insures the survival of the fittest in every department.**[127]

In his article *Darwin's Three Mistakes*, the evolutionary scientist Kenneth J. Hsü, reveals the Darwinist thoughts of America's foremost capitalists:

> Darwinism was also used in a defense of competitive individualism and its economic corollary of laissez-faire capitalism in England and in America. Andrew Carnegie wrote that the "law of competition, be it benign or not, is here; we cannot evade it." Rockefeller went a step further when he claimed that "the growth of a large business is merely a survival of the fittest; it is merely the working out of a law of nature."[128]

PEOPLE SLEEPING IN THE STREETS

Poor people left on the streets in a wealthy and comfortable country...

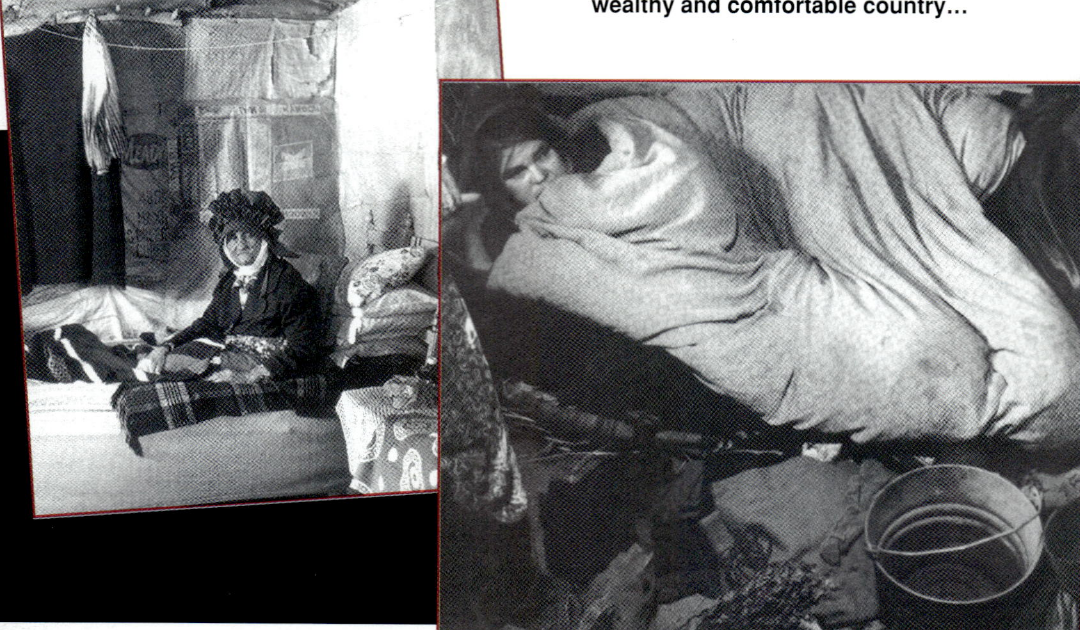

It is exceedingly interesting that in America foundations such as the Rockefeller Foundation and the Carnegie Institution, founded by great capitalist dynasties such as Rockefeller and Carnegie, should give important financial support to research into evolution.

As has been seen from what has been explained so far, capitalism has dragged human beings to worship only money and the power that comes from money. By counting all kinds of religious and ethical values as nothing, societies influenced by evolutionary suggestions began to give importance to material power, and moved away from such feelings as compassion, mercy, and sacrifice.

This capitalist morality holds sway in almost all societies in our day. For this reason the poor, the helpless, and the crippled are denied charity, and are not looked out for or protected. Even if they fall victim to the most serious and lethal disease they are unable to find any body or humane aid to protect and help them recover. The poor man is left to his sickness and to death. In many countries such unjust and inhumane practices as little children ruthlessly being made to work and being left without any social rights are frequently encountered.

Today the reason for countries such as Ethiopia falling victim to drought and starvation is the dominance of this capitalist morality. While aid and support from many countries could save these hungry people, they are abandoned to starvation and poverty.

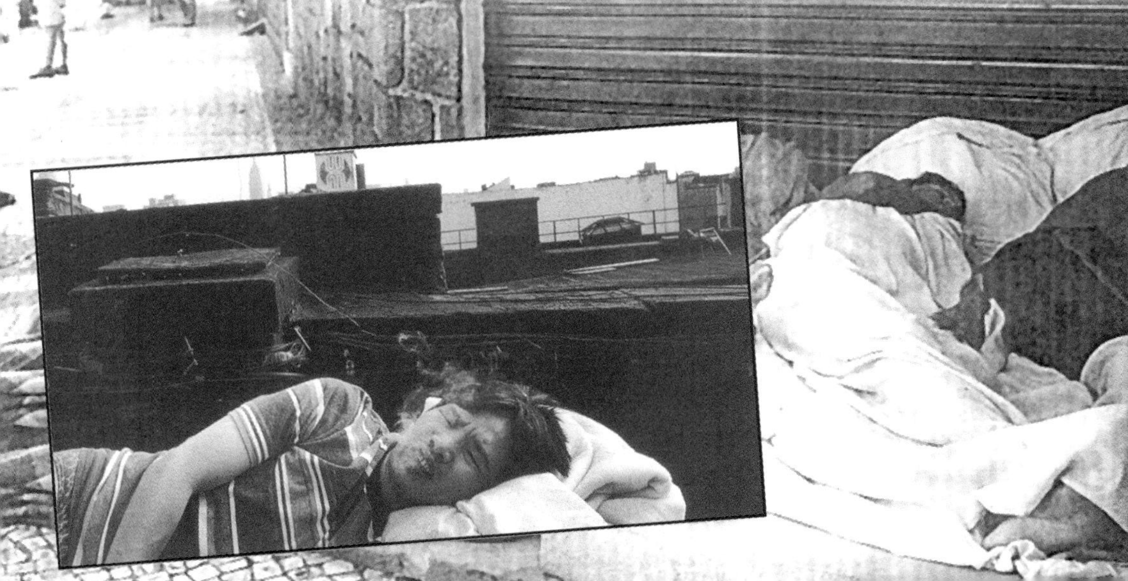

Another feature of capitalist society is the way it gives room to inequality within itself. In societies of this kind the divide between rich and poor grows ever wider, as the poor grow poorer, the wealth of the rich grows greater. The existence of millions of homeless people and these people being left to live in the most inhumane conditions, even in America, the most highly developed country in the world, is a result of capitalist morality. Of course American society is wealthy enough to protect all these people and find them jobs. But because the prevailing mentality is not to let the poor rise, but to rise by treading on the poor, no solution is offered to these people. This is the result of the putting into practice of the Social Darwinists' claims that "In order to rise there has to be a stepping stone for one to tread on."

At this juncture, attention has to be drawn to an important point: Throughout history there have always been societies where the poor and weak were trodden down, where only material things were important, and where selfishness, self-interest, and cheating were seen as the only way to become rich: in the past too there lived people who thought only

material things were of any worth and who were far removed from the features of any pleasing morality. But from the second half of the 19th century people with such views entered a very different period. For the last 150 years people and societies which possess this ruthless make-up have begun not to be condemned or criticised like the others. Behaviour of this sort began at last to be accepted as a law of nature. And at this point Darwinism had become a false religion justifying immorality and pitilessness.

Robert E. D. Clark explains the situation this way:

Evolution, in short, gave the doer of evil a respite from his conscience. The most unscrupulous behaviour towards a competitor could not be rationalized; evil could be called good.[129]

And H. Enoch wrote in his book *Evolution or Creation*:

Prof J. Holmes says, "Darwinism consistently applied would measure goodness in terms of survival value"... This is the law of the jungle where "might is right", and the fittest survive. Whether cunning and cruelty, cowardice or deceit, whatever will enable the individual to survive is good and right for that individual or that society. [130]

PEOPLE SUFFERING FROM HUNGER

Although today there are considerable resources in the world, millions of children are abandoned to starve because of the capitalist mentality.

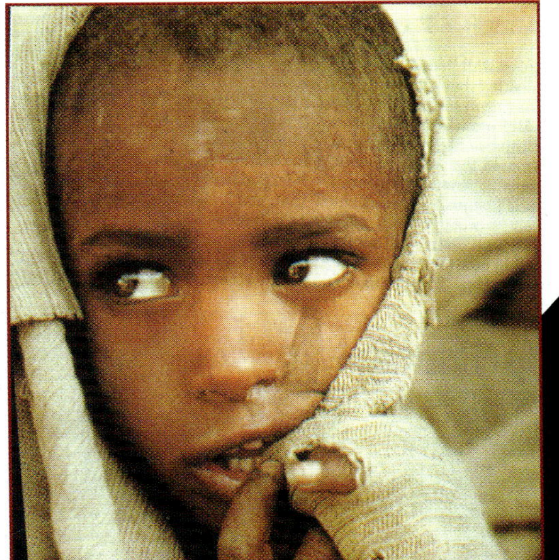

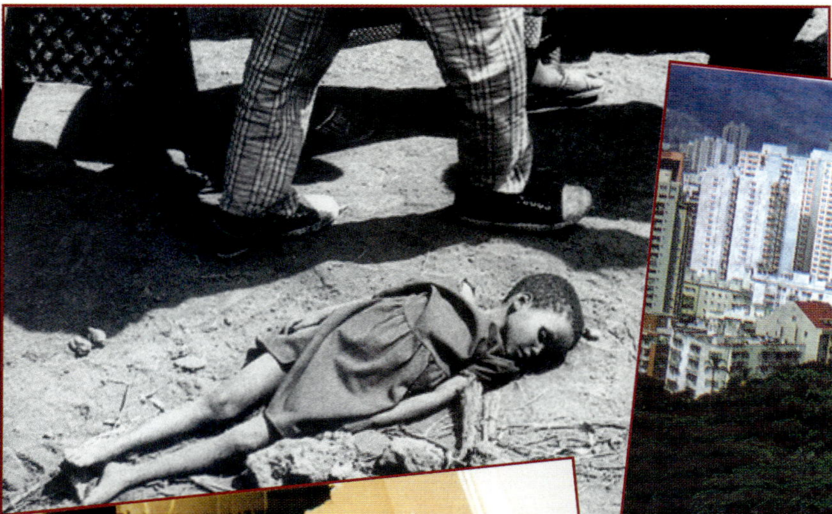

*The beggar and the destitute had
some right to their wealth.
(Surat adh-Dhariyat: 19)*

Poverty isn't defined merely by GDP. It has political and educational causes, and multidimensional remedies.

WILL THERE BE ANY HOPE FOR THE POOR?

BY AMARTYA SEN

PROGRESS IS MORE PLAUSIBLY JUDGED BY THE REDUCTION OF DEPRIVATION THAN by the further enrichment of the opulent. We cannot really have an adequate understanding of the future without some view about how well the lives of the poor can be expected to go. Is there, then, hope for the poor? To answer this question, we need an understanding of who should count as poor. Some types of poverty are easy enough to identify. There is no way of escaping immediate diagnosis when faced with what King Lear called "loop'd and window'd raggedness."

'We Ask People for Anything to Eat'

The strong steal from the weak, and the weak fight each other in a bid to survive in Somalia

BY JEFFREY BARTHOLET

Abdu Hassan Ibrahim and his family are on the road to Mogadishu, baking in the midday sun. A rusty sword is their only protection, a dry piece of goat hide their only food. Ibrahim pulls the rag shirt off his back to show the marks where thugs in the town of Baidoa whipped him with switches. His sister Hawa looks on, all bones and eyes. One of her children, emaciated and coughing, plops to the ground. "We are searching for something to eat," pleads Hawa, 35, who lost her husband to starvation three months ago. "We ask people for anything to eat." The family still has to walk across 100 miles of thorny scrubland before they reach the capital, where they hope to find food. Trucks bristling with guns honk as they speed past. Down the road, birds peck at the carcass of another traveler who didn't make it.

If Ibrahim's plight seems unremittingly sad, consider this: if he had a little money, he could buy some of the American rice available in some places for about 25 cents a kilo—scooped out of bags marked NOT TO BE SOLD OR EXCHANGED. Drought and civil war are no longer the only killers in Somalia. Now shameless capitalists are adding to the climbing death toll, undermining the hard work of Somalis trying to save their starving compatriots. Looters have stolen hundreds of tons of donated food, and much of it is stockpiled in warehouses by merchants. Some businessmen in Somalia are making huge profits importing khat, the leafy stimulant chewed by virtually anyone who has a gun and a craving to get high. Others have reaped hard currency by exporting Somalia's infrastructure, literally: whole factories have been dismantled and shipped abroad. "There are still Somalis who are helping the people," says Oker Ali, a 39-year-old Somali working for Concern, the Irish charity. "But too many others are making a profit from the situation."

Extortion is now an accepted business practice. Irish Concern workers in Mogadishu were held hostage for more than 24 hours last week by their own drivers and guards after Somali contractors demanded more money. "Unless we get paid what others get paid, no one comes in, no one goes out," snapped a gunman at the Concern office. The issue was finally resolved after senior United Nations officials intervened, along with members of the United Somali Congress (USC) militia that ostensibly controls the area. In the end, Concern agreed to give drivers and guards a small lunch allowance. "There are some real bastards out

Hundreds wait in the sun for a ladle of...

NEWSWEEK/SEPTEMBER 7

Those among you possessing resources and other means should not fail to give (something to) near relatives, paupers and those who are refugees for Allah's sake; let them act forgivingly and show indulgence. Do you not like Allah to pardon you? Allah is Forgiving, Merciful. (Surat an-Nur: 22)

WORLD AFFAIRS

The Road to Hell

Racked by civil war and famine, Somalia depends on aid from the outside world for its survival. But how far can international intervention go?

BY JEFFREY BARTHOLET

I can't stand up," mutters Yussef Sheik Hussein, ignoring the swirl of flies attracted to a half-dozen dying Somali nearby. "Do you have some medicine?" Hussein's emaciated body seems

famished farmers will eat donated seeds instead of sowing them. Rain will, however, reach thousands of corpses planted in shallow graves and drench open latrines, raising fears of major cholera and typhoid epidemics. That would be the final blow to a country already dependent on the outside

As we have seen, lack of religion and the Darwinism which inspired it lay behind all the people, systems, and ideologies which have brought worry, difficulty, pain, and hopelessness to the world, particularly in the last 150 years. Those who thought that they could protect their own interests in the selfish and ruthless environment brought about by lack of religion saw Darwinism as a saviour for themselves. They adopted Darwinism's thesis of "the weak disappear as the strong live" as a philosophy of life for themselves.

They were not aware of it, but these people who thought they were preparing a great trap for all of mankind, actually prepared it for themselves. Because no matter how much they struggle to survive and stay alive, there is actually one judge, one lord, and one Master, whether of themselves, of the whole world, of everything they try to possess, the leaders they bind themselves to, or the ideologies and "isms" they believe in. Allah is the one judge and power. And not the temporary power and opportunities given to human beings, the things they gain so ruthlessly by struggle and oppressing other people, by the sweat of their own brows. The wealth, strength, and power which a human being thinks he gains by himself are actually given to him by Allah to try him. No matter how much he may believe that he is in an arena of struggle where the weak are eliminated and the strong conquer, in actual fact every human being is living a test set by Allah for himself. Allah reveals in a holy verse that he tries human beings by means of the opportunities he gives them:

We made everything on the earth adornment for it so that We could test them to see whose actions are the best. (Surat al-Kahf: 7)

Those who think that they have won what they possess as the result of a "fight for survival" will feel a heart-rending pain for which there is no compensation, and great sorrow when they come face to face to face with reality in the hereafter and see what an empty idea they followed:

The Companions of the Garden will call out to the Companions of the Fire, 'We have found that what our Lord promised us is true. Have you found that what your Lord promised you is true?' They will say, 'Yes, we have!' Between them a herald will proclaim: 'May the curse of Allah be on

the wrongdoers those who bar access to the Way of Allah, desiring to make it crooked, and reject the hereafter.' .... The Companions of the Ramparts will call out to men they recognise by their mark, saying, 'What you amassed was of no use to you, nor was your arrogance. (Surat al-A'raf: 44-5, 48)

As for those who have not been influenced by Darwinist-capitalist thinking and who have not forgotten the reason for their being in the world and the existence of Allah, they see other human beings as living things created by Allah. As Allah has ordered them, they always treat other human beings pleasantly, feel affection and compassion, and do everything that they possibly can to take away their difficulties and worries. They always speak the pleasantest words, look after the orphaned, help the sick and crippled, and protect and watch after them. People like this avoid sin and keep their duties to Allah as it is revealed in the Qur'an and are the most superior in Allah's sight: they pay no attention to wealth, race, colour, class, ideology, or philosophy.

The greatest catastrophe visited by Darwinism upon mankind was without doubt to turn people away from religion. A violent moral and spiritual collapse swiftly comes to societies which turn away from religion. There are many examples of this in societies in our day.

At this point some people will say that Darwinism cannot be held responsible for peoples' lack of religion because a large number of those people who live a life without religion have never heard of the claims of Darwinism. The second part of this objection is true. These days the number of people who defend Darwinism in a knowledgeable way is limited. But this restricted minority are people who direct society's ideas in most fields. The influence they have developed on society reaches countless people. They have the possibility of imposing their world view on a large section of society. For instance, the best-known university professors, a large part of famous cinema directors, and editors of world-famous publishing houses, newspapers, and magazines are for the most part evolutionists, and therefore naturally atheists. For which reason, the parts of society they address are affected by them and influenced by their evolutionary and anti-religious thinking. As a result, societies emerge where these perverse ideas are widely accepted.

Ernst Mayr, a Harvard University biologist and one of the world's foremost evolutionists, describes the place of the theory of evolution in the life of society in these words:

> Since Darwin, every knowing person agrees that man is descended from the apes… Evolution has an impact on every aspect of man's thinking: his philosophy, his metaphysics, his ethics…[131]

Darwinists' wide-ranging dominance over the life of society acts like a powerful form of "hypnosis" on people. A large part of the younger generation in particular, with not enough experience of life to form any world view, even a very superficial one, can easily be taken in by suggestions of this type. It is exceedingly easy to bring these people to have the desired thought processes through the magazines they read, the films, plays or music clips they watch, and, most important of all, the education they receive in schools. For this influence is the reason that people have believed the theory of evolution to be true for 150 years, despite its deceptions and unscientific nature.

If you notice, anti-religious propaganda is seldom carried out openly these days, nobody openly suggests that anyone should have no religion. But for this reason covert methods are employed, imperceptible at first sight. Mockery of religion, religious subjects, or people known for their religious faith, and the use of words which mean the rejection of God, destiny, and religion in song lyrics, novels, films, newspaper headlines, and jokes, are just a few of these covert methods.

The subjects of Darwinism, on the other hand, are the most common tools of anti-religious propaganda. In even the most unconnected subjects the lie that our ancestors were monkeys is stressed. The claims of the theory of evolution are even written between the lines in human psychological analysis. In this way, human societies emerge which treat religion, the afterlife, and moral responsibilities lightly, which do not think, which do not fear God, and which do not really believe in Him, even if, when asked, they say that they do believe in God and religion. People who have no faith or fear of Allah, know no limits in any matter, and begin to live like the animals they think their ancestors were.

For example, one cannot expect people who are incautious and who do not fear Allah to protect their chastity because they think there is no limit they have to observe. They become willing to perform any kind of immorality as long as they can do it out of other people's sight. Just as in our day, especially among the young and definite sections of society, the ever-further pushing of limits, the spreading of an understanding which counts moral values and God's edicts as nothing, and people's turning away from religion as a result of the suggestions of Darwinism, are one outcome of this. People who see themselves as left completely unrestricted and who believe that they will not have to account to anyone, demonstrate an ever-increasing profligacy with every passing day. Young men or women can make statements to newspapers describing their sex lives in the tiniest detail, and the newspapers publish them, and the readers do not mind. Adultery, which the media praise and describe with great care, and even call everybody to commit, has come to be a deed that nobody finds the least out of the ordinary. Under careful examination, behind murder, prostitution, cheating, and swindling of all kinds, giving and taking bribes, and telling lies: in short at the base of all immoral behaviour the lack of religion is to be seen. The most effective way this lack of religion is spread is the violent influence of Darwin's lie that "the human being emerged as a result of sheer coincidence."

Ken Ham, the author of the book *The Lie: Evolution*, takes the lack of religion which Darwinism gave rise to as a subject and says:

> If you reject God and replace Him with another belief that puts chance, random processes in the place of God, there is no basis for right or wrong. Rules become whatever you want to make them. There are no absolutes—no principles that must be adhered to. People will write their own rules.[132]

The well-known evolutionist Theodious Dobzhansky agrees that the idea of "natural selection," the foundation of Darwinism, gives rise to a morally degenerate society:

> Natural selection can favor egotism, hedonism, cowardice instead of bravery, cheating and exploitation, while group ethics in virtually all societies tend to counteract or forbid such 'natural' behavior, and to glorify their opposites: kindness, generosity, and even self-sacrifice for the good of others of one's tribe or nation and finally of mankind.[133]

If we look around us today, we can immediately see the traces of the deep and most important devastation wrought by Darwinist morality. The idea that progress, development, and civilisation are the result of people living separate from one another and with no ties of mutual assistance, devotion, respect, and affection, is imposed upon societies. The suggestion that such a result has to be accepted for greater production and development is frequently made. Whereas this is a result of human beings bringing themselves to the "status of animals," not of development and civilisation.

The truth is that man is not a species of animal and did not come into existence from any animal. Man, whom God created with the possession of reason, intelligence, conscience, and a soul, is a completely different creature from other living things by virtue of these qualities. But under the influence of the spell of Darwinist-materialist morality, human beings forget these qualities and stoop to pettiness, immorality and a lack of conscience and consciousness not even seen in animals. Then they say, "We are in any case descended from animals, these are also a genetic inheritance from them," and prepare a so-called scientific basis for their own lack of willpower and consciousness.

Many Darwinist behavioural scientists take this logic as a starting point, and claim that human beings' demonstrating a tendency to crime is an inheritance from their animal forefathers. The famous evolutionist Stephen Jay Gould puts this claim, first suggested by the Italian physicist Lombroso, forward in the following manner in his book *Ever Since Darwin*.

> Biological theories of criminality were scarcely new, but Lombroso gave the argument a novel, evolutionary twist. Born criminals are not simply deranged or diseased; they are, literally, throwbacks to a previous evolutionary stage. The hereditary characters of our primitive and apish ancestors remain in our genetic repertoire. Some unfortunate men are born with an unusually large number of these ancestral characters. Their behavior may have been appropriate in savage societies of the past; today, we brand it as criminal. We may pity the born criminal, for he cannot help himself; but we cannot tolerate his actions.[134]

According to the claims of the Darwinists, in other words, a human being's killing another, his causing him pain, stealing, and starting fights, are a genetically transferred inheritance from his apish ancestors. For which reason, according to this claim, these crimes do not belong to that person and are seen as excusable.

As can be seen from these claims, Darwinist thinking counts human beings' conscience and willpower, and such skills as reason and judgement, as nothing, and accepts that man is an unintelligent creature, who behaves according to instinct, just like animals. According to this view, just as a wild lion cannot prevent the aggression within him and cannot exhibit virtuous behaviour such as overcoming his anger, or showing forgiveness and patience, so man behaves in the same manner. It is evident that there will be a lack of peace and security, disorder, conflict, and fighting in a society which shelters such people.

The Ruthless and Pessimistic Living Model Proposed to Mankind by Darwinism

According to the Darwinists and materialists, the whole universe, human beings included, is the work of chaos and coincidences. As the influence of this view grows in society, there emerge irresponsible people who believe themselves to be totally unrestricted.

A person who has no purpose does not think, cannot form the aim of developing himself, is uncaring, mocking, is unfeeling, affected by nothing, cannot use his conscience, and recognises no rules or limits. He can possess no virtue or finer quality. In his own perverse view, as a developed animal himself, in this world he must look for food and reproduce, in the same way as other living creatures, and after meeting certain needs must find as much entertainment and enjoyment as possible and wait for death. And it can be seen that, even though most people are unaware of the details of Darwinism, they live the life that Darwinism foresaw for mankind.

Because they live a life which is ruthless and which will eventually come to an end, these people are carried away by great depression, pessimism, and hopelessness. The thought that everything will end with death and become as nothing causes these people to be unhappy and shut up within themselves. One of the reasons behind suicides, psychological problems, and depressions is the negatives effects of the Darwinist spell on human psychology.

Richard Dawkins, one of the fiercest defenders of evolution of our times, reveals one example of this. Dawkins claims that human beings are gene machines and that the only reason for their existence is to pass these genes on to subsequent generations. In Dawkins' view there is no other purpose to either the universe's or man's existence. All the universe and human beings are the products of chaos and coincidence. People who are deceived by such a claim easily fall prey to depression and hopelessness. He who believes that the only point to life is to pass on his genes, and that everything ends with death, that nothing he does in the world has any meaning, who thinks that friendship, love, goodness, and beauty have no value, will think that life is pitiless and unnecessary and will be able to take no pleasure from anything. In the foreword to his book *Unweaving the Rainbow*, Dawkins admits the negative and pessimistic effect his claim regarding the point of human life has on people:

> A foreign publisher of my first book confessed that **he could not sleep for three nights** after reading it, so troubled was he by what he saw as its **cold, bleak message**. Others have asked me how I can bear to get up in the mornings. A teacher from a distant country wrote to me reproachfully that a pupil had come to him in tears after reading the same book, because it had persuaded her that life was empty and purposeless. He advised her not to show the book to any of her friends, for fear of contaminating them with the same **nihilistic pessimism**. Similar accusations of barren desolation, of promoting an arid and joyless message, are frequently flung at science in general, and it is easy for scientists to play up to them. My colleague Peter Atkins begins his book The Second Law (1984) in this vein:
>
> We are the children of chaos, and the deep structure of change is decay. **At root, there is only corruption, and the unstemmable tide of chaos. Gone is purpose**; all that is left is direction. **This is the bleakness we have to accept** as we peer deeply and dispassionately into the heart of the Universe.[135]

Another Darwinist who proposed that life is nothing and caused life to be looked at pessimistically, was the German philosopher Nietzsche, whose theses of racial superiority provided a philosophical support for

Hitler. The thought Nietzsche put forward, known as "nihilism" or "nothingism" is basically this: Man must have a reason for living. But this purpose, according to Nietzsche who denied the existence of God, has nothing to do with God's having created man. For this reason, in Nietzsche's philosophy, man constantly seeks a purpose but is unable to find one and experiences the pessimism and hopelessness born of this. The right thing is to seek the purpose behind man's existence. But if, like Nietzsche, a person absolutely rejects the fundamental purpose and starts to look for a purpose outside the scope of this truth, then of course he is not going to be able to find it. And let us add here that Nietzsche died mad.

Societies which forget that they were created by God for a purpose are inevitably condemned to undergo a moral and spiritual collapse. Wealth, welfare, and economic development in no way bring these people peace and security. Many things push people who fail to comply with the commands of reason and conscience, and who see themselves as unrestricted and purposeless creatures, to unhappiness, hopelessness, and pessimism. The most important thing is the sorrow, unhappiness and pessimism that these people, who think that they will cease to exist with death, will feel when they see the true life that they will meet after death.

Whereas a person who believes in God and the hereafter is aware of what an important outcome he is living for. He always bears the joy and hope of winning the mercy of God and paradise. Whatever happens he gives thanks to God: for which reason he never falls prey to hopelessness and pessimism.

CONCLUSION

THE SWAMP OF DARWINISM MUST BE DRAINED

All through history there have been wars, oppression, killings, and conflict. But the reason for the number and range of these disasters being so great in the last century is the false veil of scientific justification that Darwinism lent to this killing, oppression and conflict. Because Darwinism's totally erroneous claims about nature ran parallel to the pronunciations of these ideologies, assassins, dictators, and sadistic ideologues were able to try to demonstrate that they were right and justified by saying "the law of nature also applies to society" regarding their policies.

In our day the theory of evolution is still defended for philosophical and ideological reasons. The colonialism which exploded with the theory of evolution in the 19th century, Nazi Germany, and the Soviet Union are now things of the past. But the Darwinist-materialist philosophy which was their ultimate foundation is still vigorously defended by certain circles, and the destructive effects of this philosophy still continue to be felt all over the world.

Despite the fact that he is an evolutionist, Kenneth J. Hsü has written in this way about the disasters that Darwinism has led to for mankind:

> We were victims of a cruel social ideology that assumes that competition among individuals, classes, nations or races is **the natural condition of life, and that it is also natural for the superior to dispossess the inferior...** The law of natural selection is not, I will maintain, science. It is an ideology, and a wicked one...[136]

Of course judicial and physical precautions must be taken. But these precautions can only cover up the wounds brought about by those ideologies. The permanent solution lies in a cultural and scientific treatment.

With the collapse of Darwinism from the cultural and scientific point of view, those philosophies which draw strength from it will also disappear, and this will mean the lifting of oppression from the world.

For this reason a heavy responsibility falls to those who possess conscience and faith, who have knowledge of spiritual values. It is not right to ignore or underestimate the disasters which Darwinism visited upon the world, particularly in the last century, and the suffering that people and societies underwent. Everyone who grasps the urgency of the matter must do what he can for a cultural attack to bring an end to this deception, which has lasted for 150 years.

The only thing that can bring an end to this deception in the true sense, which can bring a solution to the fundamental question which mankind lives, is the life of the morality of the Qur'an. These disasters will come to an end as people turn to the true religion, when the beauty, love, affection, compassion, justice, devotion, co-operation, and tolerance which the Qur'an brings to peoples' lives are widely lived. As one of Allah's holy verses has revealed, "truth will come" and "falsehood will vanish:"

> **Say: 'Truth has come and falsehood has vanished. Falsehood is always bound to vanish.' (Surat al-Isra: 81)**

THE MISCONCEPTION OF EVOLUTION

Darwinism, or rather the theory of evolution, is nothing but an unscientific fallacy, proposed with the purpose of denying the truth of creation, in which it has not succeeded. This theory, which claims that life came about non-organic matter by a series of coincidences, has basically been discredited with the emergence of the fact that the universe was created by God. It is God Who created the universe and ordered it, down to the tiniest detail. In this case it is not possible for the theory of evolution, which claims that living things were not created by God, but that they were the result of coincidences, to be true.

In fact, when we study the theory of evolution, we see that really it is denied by scientific discoveries. The structure that exists in life is much more complex and striking than that in the non-living world. For example we can examine by what sensitive balances atoms are ordered in the non-living world, and furthermore in what complicated structures these atoms are brought together in the living world, and we can study what extraordinary mechanisms are formed by using them, such as proteins, enzymes, and cells.

So this extraordinary structure in life has invalidated the theory of evolution at the end of the 20th century.

We have considered this subject in great detail in others of our studies and are still continuing to so do. But because of its importance it will be useful to recapitulate it here.

The Difficulties that Demolish Darwin's Theory

The theory of evolution, a teaching whose history goes back to Ancient Greece, was fully set out in the middle of the 19th century. The most important development which placed the theory on the agenda of the world of science was the book *The Origin of Species*, published by Charles Darwin in 1859. In this book Darwin came out against different species of living creature in the world being individually created by God. According to Darwin all species came from a common ancestor and had grown different from each other by small changes over time.

Darwin's theory was based on no solid scientific discovery: as he accepted himself, it was just a "progression of logic." In fact, as Darwin admitted in a long section in his book under the heading, **"The Difficulties On Theory,"** the theory had no answer to a number of important questions.

Darwin hoped that the difficulties facing his theory would be overcome as science developed in time and that new scientific discoveries would reinforce it. But, in total contrast to Darwin's hopes, the development of science left the fundamental claims of the theory, one by one, unfounded.

Darwinism's defeat in the face of science can be studied under three basic headings:

1. The theory is quite unable to explain how life emerged in the world for the first time.

2. There is no scientific evidence to show that the "evolutionary mechanisms" proposed by the theory really possess any evolutionary effects.

3. The fossil record presents a picture in total opposition to the theory's expectations.

In this section we shall examine the main lines of each heading.

The First Insurmountable Obstacle: The Origin of Life

The theory of evolution claims that all living species came from one living cell, which emerged in the primitive world some 3.8 billion years ago. How it was that one single cell formed millions of complex living species, and if such a form of evolution did happen, why not traces of it have been found in the fossil record, are questions that the theory has been unable to explain. But before all that, we must stop at the first step of this alleged period of evolution. How did this alleged "first cell" come about?

Because the theory of evolution rejects creation and accepts no supernatural intervention, it claims that that "first cell" came about, with no structure, plan, or order, by coincidence within the laws of nature. In other words, according to the theory, non-living matter must have produced a living cell as a result of coincidences. Yet this is a claim which flies in the face of the most basic known biological laws.

"Life Comes From Life"

Darwin did not mention the subject of the origin of life in his book. Because of the primitive scientific understanding of his day, he assumed that living things possessed a very simple structure. According to the theory called "spontaneous generation," which had been believed in since the Middle Ages, it was believed that non-living substances could come together by chance and form a living creature. At that time it was a common belief that insects were formed by leftover food and mice from wheat. Interesting experiments were done to try and prove it. A little wheat was spread over a dirty rag, and it was thought that after waiting for a bit mice would emerge from the combination.

Meat becoming maggot-ridden was counted as proof that life could emerge from non-living substances. Whereas it was later understood that maggots did not emerge by themselves from the surface of meat, but that they emerged from larva, smaller than the eye can see, which flies brought and left there.

At the time when Darwin wrote *The Origin of Species*, the belief that bacteria could emerge from inorganic matter saw wide acceptance in the world of science.

Whereas five years after the publication of Darwin's book, the famous French biologist Louis Pasteur definitively destroyed this belief, which was the basis of evolution. As a result of his long research and studies Pasteur summed up the results he had arrived at by saying, "The claim that inanimate matter can originate life is buried in history for good."[137]

The defenders of the theory of evolution resisted Pasteur's findings for a long time. Yet as science developed and revealed the complicated structure of the living cell, the invalidity of the claim that life could come about by itself became even more obvious.

The Unproductive Struggles of the 20th Century

In the 20th century the first evolutionist to take in hand the subject of the origin of life was the well-known Russian biologist Alexander Oparin. In a number of theses he put forward in the 1930s, Oparin attempted to prove that the living cell could come about by coincidence. But these efforts were to end in failure, and Oparin would have to make this confession, **"Unfortunately, the origin of the cell remains a question which is actually the darkest point of the entire evolution theory."[138]**

Evolutionists who followed Oparin's path tried to carry out experiments that would lead to a solution to the origin of life. The best-known of these experiments was carried out in 1953 by the famous American chemist Stanley Miller. Miller brought together the gasses, which he claimed were in the earth's primitive atmosphere in experimental conditions, added energy to the mixture, and synthesised a few organic molecules (amino-acids) used in the production of proteins.

The invalidity of that experiment, which in those years was regarded as an important step in the name of evolution, and that the atmosphere used in the experiment was very different from the conditions of the real world, emerged in the years that followed.[139]

After a long silence, Miller himself admitted that the atmospheric environment employed was not realistic.[140]

All the evolutionary efforts throughout the 20th century to explain the question of the origin of life ended in failure. The well-known geochemist Jeffrey Bada, from the Scripps Institute in San Diego, accepts this truth in an article published in 1998 in the evolutionist magazine *Earth*:

> Today as we leave the twentieth century, **we still face the biggest unsolved problem** that we had when we entered the twentieth century: **How did life originate on Earth?**[141]

Life's Complex Structure

The principle reason for the theory of evolution's being in such a great difficulty as regards the origin of life, is the fact that even those living things which are thought of as having the very simplest structures actually have unbelievably complicated structures. The living cell is more complicated than all of the technological products made by mankind. To such an extent that not even the most highly developed laboratories in the world can bring inorganic substances together and produce a living cell.

The conditions necessary for a cell to appear are many more than can be explained by coincidences. The probability of proteins, the building blocks of cell, being synthesized coincidenctally, is 1 in 10^{950} for an average protein made up of 500 amino acids. In mathematics, a probability smaller than 1 over 10^{50} is practically considered to be impossible.

As for the DNA molecule, which lies in the nucleus of the cell and contains genetic information, that is an unbelievable data bank. If a human being's genetic code were to be set down on paper it would fill a library of 900 volumes of 500 pages each.

And here there is another most interesting point to add: DNA can only replicate with the help of some specialized proteins (enzymes). However, the synthesis of these enzymes can only be realised by the information coded in DNA. As they depend on each other, they have to exist at the same time for replication. This brings the scenario that life originated by itself to a deadlock. The well-known evolutionist professor Leslie Orgel, from San Diego California University, admits this truth in the October 1994 edition of *Scientific American* magazine:

> It is extremely improbable that proteins and nucleic acids, both of which are structurally complex, arose spontaneously in the same place at the same ti-

me. Yet it also seems impossible to have one without the other. And so, at first glance, one might have to conclude that life could never, in fact, have originated by chemical means.[142]

There is no doubt that if it is impossible for life to come about through natural effects, then one must accept that life was "created" in a supernatural way. This truth openly invalidates the theory of evolution, the basic aim of which is to deny creation.

The Imaginary Mechanisms of Evolution

The second major point which invalidates Darwin's theory is the fact that it has been realised that the two concepts put forward by the theory as "evolutionary mechanisms" actually possess no evolutionary force.

Darwin had totally linked the claim of evolution which he put forward to "natural selection." The importance he attached to this mechanism can be clearly seen from the title of his book: *The Origin of Species, By Means of Natural Selection...*

It is based on the idea that in the struggle for survival in nature living creatures which are strong and adapted to the natural conditions will survive. For example, when a herd of deer is threatened by beasts of prey, those deer which can run the fastest will survive. In this way the herd will consist of fast and powerful individuals. But of course this mechanism does not make deer evolve, it cannot turn them into another species, for example horses.

For this reason the mechanism of natural selection possesses no evolutionary force. Darwin was aware of this fact, and in *The Origin of Species* he was forced to say:

Natural selection can do nothing until favourable variations chance to occur.[143]

The Influence of Lamarck

So, how did these "favourable variations" come about? Within the primitive scientific understanding of his time, Darwin tried to base the answer to this question on Lamarck. According to the French biologist Lamarck, who lived before Darwin, living things pass on physical changes which they undergo during the course of their lives to subsequent generations, and new species emerge as a result of these properties which are amassed from generation to generation. For example, in Lamarck's view, giraffes developed from antelopes, whose necks had grown longer from generation to generation as they struggled to eat the leaves on tall trees.

Darwin gave similar examples, for instance he claimed in *The Origin of Species* that some bears which entered the water to find food turned in time into whales.[144]

But the laws of inheritance, which Mendel discovered and which was proven with the development of genetic science in the 20th century, destroyed the myth that acquired traits can be passed on to later generations. In this way, **natural selection was a "one off," and for that reason a completely ineffective mechanism.**

Neo-Darwinism and Mutations

In order to find a solution in this situation the Darwinists put forward the "Modern Synthetic Theory," or Neo-Darwinism, as it is more widely known, at the end of the 1930s. Alongside natural selection, Neo-Darwinism added as a "reason for favourable variations," mutations, or defects in the genes of living creatures as a result of external influences such as radiation of duplication errors.

And still today in the world the model which defends its validity in the name of evolution is Neo-Darwinism. The theory maintains that the millions of living species in the world emerged as a result of mutations, or genetic defects over time, in these living creatures' countless complex organs, such as ears, eyes, lungs, and wings. But there is a scientific fact which disarms the theory: **Mutations do not develop living creatures, on the contrary, they always damage them.**

The reason for this is very simple. DNA has a very complex structure. Any chance alteration in the molecule only leads to damage. The American geneticist B. G. Ranganathan explains it this way:

> **Mutations are small, random, and harmful.** They rarely occur and the best possibility is that they will be ineffectual. These four characteristics of mutations imply that mutations cannot lead to an evolutionary development. A random change in a highly specialised organism is either ineffectual or harmful. A random change in a watch cannot improve the watch. It will most probably harm it or at best be ineffectual. An earthquake does not improve the city, it brings destruction.[145]

As a matter of fact no example of a useful mutation, in other words one which developed genetic science, has so far been observed. It has been seen that all mutations are harmful. It has been realised that the theory of evolution's mutations, which it suggested as "evolutionary mechanisms," are actually a genetic event which only destroy and cripple living creatures. (The commonest mutation seen in human beings is cancer). Of course a destructive mechanism cannot be an "evolutionary mechanism." Natural selection, as Darwin had accepted, "can do nothing by itself." This truth shows us that there is no "evolutionary mechanism" in nature. And since there is no evolutionary mechanism, the imaginary period called evolution cannot have existed.

The Fossil Record: No Sign of Intermediate Forms

The clearest proof that the scenario of the theory of evolution did not happen is the fossil record.

According to the theory of evolution, living creatures arose from each other. A previously existing species turned into another over time and all species emerged in this way. According to the theory, this change covered a period of millions of years and moved forward step by step.

This being the case, countless "intermediate species" should have emerged and lived over this alleged period of change.

For example, in the past, although fish still bore their own features, they must also have gained some features of reptiles, and half-fish half-reptile creatures must have lived. Or, while still possessing the features of reptiles, they must also have taken on some of the features of birds, and reptile-birds must have emerged. These, because they were in a period of transformation, must have been sickly, incomplete, and faulty creatures. Evolutionists call these creatures which they believe must have lived in the past **"intermediate forms."**

If creatures of this type really did live in the past, their numbers and varieties must have been in the millions. And the remains of these highly peculiar creatures should be met in the fossil record. In *The Origin of Species*, Darwin explained it this way:

> If my theory be true, **numberless intermediate varieties**, linking most closely all of the species of the same group together **must assuredly have existed...** Consequently, evidence of their former existence could be found only amongst fossil remains.[146]

Darwin's Vanishing Hopes

However, despite fossil research being feverishly carried out in all parts of the from the middle of the 19th century to the present, intermediate forms have not so far been found. All the discoveries found in the excavations and research, far from showing what the evolutionists were expecting, have revealed that living creatures emerged suddenly, all intact, and complete.

The famous British palaeontologist (fossil expert) Derek W. Ager, admits this, despite being an evolutionist:

> The point emerges that if we examine the fossil record in detail, whether at the level of orders or of species, we find — over and over again — **not gradual evolution, but the sudden explosion of one group at the expense of another.**[147]

In other words, in the fossil record, all species of living creature emerged suddenly and in their finished form, with no intermediate form between them. This is the exact opposite of what Darwin foresaw. Furthermore, this is a very strong proof that living species were created. Because the only explanation for a living species' emerging flawless and suddenly, with no ancestor for it to have evolved from, must be that that species was created. This truth is accepted by the well-known evolutionist biologist Douglas Futuyma:

> **Creation and evolution, between them, exhaust the possible explanations for the origin of living things.** Organisms either appeared on the earth fully developed or they did not. If they did not, they must have developed from pre-existing species by some process of modification. If they did appear in a fully developed state, they must indeed have been created by some omnipotent intelligence.[148]

Fossils reveal that living creatures emerged in the world fully and perfectly formed. In other words **the "origin of species," contrary to what Darwin thought, is creation, and not evolution.**

The Myth of the Evolution of Man

The subject most frequently brought up by defenders of the theory of evolution is the origin of man. The Darwinist claim on this subject considers that the modern human being living today descended from a number of ape-like creatures. In this period, estimated to have begun some 4-5 million years ago, it is claimed that there lived "intermediate forms" between modern man and his ancestors. In fact there are four basic "categories" in this entirely illusory scenario:

1. Australopithecus
2. Homo habilis
3. Homo erectus
4. Homo sapiens

Evolutionists give the name "Australopithecus," which means "southern ape," to man's so-called first ape-like ancestor. These living creatures were actually nothing but an extinct species of ape. Wide-ranging research by Lord Solly Zuckerman and Professor Charles Oxnard, two world-famous anatomists from Britain and the USA on Australopithecus remains shows that these living creatures belonged to an extinct species of ape and that they had no similarities to human beings.[149]

Evolutionists divide the next phase of human evolution into "homo" or human classes. According to the claim, living creatures of the "homo" series were more developed than Australopithecus. Evolutionists lay the fossils of these different living creatures back to back and make up an imaginary plan of evolution. This plan is imaginary, because in actual fact no evolutionary link between these different classes has been proven. Ernst Mayr, one of the most important defenders of the theory of evolution in the 20th century accepts this, saying "the chain reaching as far as Homo sapiens is actually lost."[150]

While writing out the plan Australopithecus>Homo habilis>Homo erectus>Homo sapiens, evolutionists say that each species was the ancestor of the one that followed. Whereas the latest discoveries by palaeontologists reveal that Australopithecus, Homo habilis, and Homo erectus lived in the same periods in different regions of the world.[151]

Furthermore, beings from the Homo erectus class survived until very recent times: Homo sapiens neandertalensis and Homo sapiens sapiens (modern man) have been found side by side in the same period.[152]

This, of course, definitely demonstrates the invalidity that these classes were one another's' ancestors. Stephen Jay Gould, one of Harvard University's palaeontologists, although himself an evolutionist, explains the dilemma in which the Darwinist theory finds itself in this way:

> What has become of our ladder if there are three coexisting lineages of hominids (A. africanus, the robust australopithecines, and H. habilis), none clearly derived from another? Moreover, none of the three display any evolutionary trends during their tenure on earth.[153]

In short, the drawings which appear in the media or in school books of imaginary "half-monkey half-man" creatures, in other words the scenario of human evolution which they are trying to keep alive just by propaganda methods, is a myth with no scientific basis.

Despite being an evolutionist, Lord Solly Zuckerman, one of Britain's most respected and well-known scientists, studied this matter for many long years, and carried out a 15-year research into Australopithecus fossils, and reached the conclusion that there was no real family tree stretching from those monkey-like creatures to man.

Zuckerman also made an interesting "spectrum of science." He drew up a "spectrum," from branches of knowledge he accepted as scientific to those he did not accept as scientific. Under Zuckerman's table the most "scientific," or in other words those based on concrete results, are chemistry and physics. After that come biological sciences, and then social sciences. At the far end of the "spectrum," that part considered most "unscientific" are, according to Zuckerman, "extrasensory perception,"— concepts such as telepathy and sixth sense and—finally "human evolution"! Zuckerman describes this end of the spectrum in this way:

> We then move right off the register of objective truth into those fields of presumed biological science, like extrasensory perception or the interpretation of man's fossil history, where to the faithful (evolutionist) anything is possible - and where the ardent believer (in evolution) is sometimes able to believe several contradictory things at the same time.[154]

Thus the myth of human evolution consists of prejudiced comments by a few people who blindly believe in the theories based on a few fossils they found.

Technology In The Eye and The Ear

Another subject that remains unanswered by evolutionary theory is the excellent quality of perception in the eye and the ear.

Before passing on to the subject of the eye, let us briefly answer the question of "how we see". Light rays coming from an object fall oppositely on the retina of the eye. Here, these light rays are transmitted into electric signals by cells and they reach a tiny spot at the back of the brain called the centre of vision. These electric signals are perceived in this centre of the brain as an image after a series of processes. With this technical background, let us do some thinking.

The brain is insulated from light. That means that the inside of the brain is solid dark, and light does not reach the location where the brain is situated. The place called the centre of vision is a solid dark place where no light ever reaches; it may even be the darkest place you have ever known. However, you observe a luminous, bright world in this pitch darkness.

The image formed in the eye is so sharp and distinct that even the technology of the 20th century has not been able to attain it. For instance, look at the book you read, your hands with which you hold it, then lift your head and look around you. Have you ever seen such a sharp and distinct image as this one at any other place? Even the most developed television screen produced by the greatest television producer in the world cannot provide such a sharp image for you. This is a three-dimensional, coloured, and extremely sharp image. For more than 100 years, thousands of engineers have been trying to achieve this sharpness. Factories, huge premises were established, much research has been done, plans and designs have been made for this purpose. Again, look at a TV screen and the book you hold in your hands. You will see that there is a big difference in sharpness and distinction. Moreover, the TV screen shows you a two-dimensional image, whereas with your eyes, you watch a three-dimensional perspective having depth.

For many years, ten of thousands of engineers have tried to make a three-dimensional TV, and reach the vision quality of the eye. Yes, they have made a three-dimensional television system but it is not possible to watch it without putting on glasses; moreover, it is only an artificial three-dimension. The background is more blurred, the foreground appears like a paper setting. Never has it been possible to produce a sharp and distinct vision like that of the eye. In both the camera and the television, there is a loss of image quality.

Evolutionists claim that the mechanism producing this sharp and distinct image has been formed by chance. Now, if somebody told you that the television in your room was formed as a result of chance, that all its atoms just happened to come together and make up this device that produces an image, what would you think? How can atoms do what thousands of people cannot?

If a device producing a more primitive image than the eye could not have been formed by chance, then it is very evident that the eye and the image seen by the eye could not have been formed by chance. The same situation applies to the ear. The outer ear picks up the available sounds by the auricle and directs them to the middle ear; the middle ear transmits the sound vibrations by intensifying them; the inner ear sends these vibrations to the brain by translating them into electric signals. Just as with the eye, the act of hearing finalises in the centre of hearing in the brain.

The situation in the eye is also true for the ear. That is, the brain is insulated from sound just like it is from light: it does not let any sound in. Therefore, no matter how noisy is the outside, the inside of the brain is completely silent. Nevertheless, the sharpest sounds are perceived in the brain. In your brain, which is insulated from sound, you listen to the symphonies of an orchestra, and hear all the noises in a crowded place. However, if the sound level in your brain was measured by a precise device at that moment, it would be seen that a complete silence is prevailing there.

As is the case with imagery, decades of effort have been spent in trying to generate and reproduce sound that is faithful to the original. The results of these efforts are sound recorders, high-fidelity systems, and systems for sensing sound. Despite all this technology and the thousands of engineers and experts who have been working on this endeavour, no sound has yet been obtained that has the same sharpness and clarity as the sound perceived by the ear. Think of the highest-quality HI-FI systems produced by the biggest company in the music industry. Even in these devices, when sound is recorded some of it is lost; or when you turn on a HI-FI you always hear a hissing sound before the music starts. However, the sounds that are the products of the technology of the human body are extremely sharp and clear. A human ear never perceives a sound accompanied by a hissing sound or with atmospherics as does HI-FI; it perceives sound exactly as it is, sharp and clear. This is the way it has been since the creation of man.

So far, no visual or recording apparatus produced by man has been as sensitive and successful in perceiving sensory data as are the eye and the ear.

However, as far as seeing and hearing are concerned, a far greater fact lies beyond all this.

To Whom Does the Consciousness that Sees and Hears Within the Brain Belong?

Who is it that watches an alluring world in its brain, listens to symphonies and the twittering of birds, and smells the rose?

The stimulations coming from the eyes, ears, and nose of a human being travel to the brain as electro-chemical nervous impulses. In biology, physiology, and biochemistry books, you can find many details about how this image forms in the brain. However, you will never come across the most important fact about this subject: Who is it that perceives these electro-chemical nervous impulses as images, sounds, odours and sensory events in the brain? There is a consciousness in the brain that perceives all this without feeling any need for eye, ear, and nose. To whom does this consciousness belong? There is no doubt that this consciousness does not belong to the nerves, the fat layer and neurons comprising the brain. This is why Darwinist-materialists, who believe that everything is comprised of matter, cannot give any answer to these questions.

For this consciousness is the spirit created by Allah. The spirit needs neither the eye to watch the images, nor the ear to hear the sounds. Furthermore, nor does it need the brain to think.

Everyone who reads this explicit and scientific fact should ponder on Almighty Allah, should fear Him and seek refuge in Him, He Who squeezes the entire universe in a pitch-dark place of a few cubic centimeters in a three-dimensional, coloured, shadowy, and luminous form.

A Materialist Belief

What we have studied so far shows that the theory of evolution is a claim openly at odds with scientific facts. The theory's claim regarding the origin life flies in the face of science, the evolutionary mechanism it proposes has no evolutionary effect, and fossils show that the necessary intermediate forms have not lived. In this case, the theory of evolution has to be jettisoned as an idea contrary to science. As a matter of fact, throughout history many ideas centred on the world, such as the evolution model, have been removed from the scientific agenda.

But the theory of evolution is being determinedly kept on the scientific agenda. Some people even try to portray criticism of the theory as "an attack on science." But why?...

The reason for this situation is that for some people the theory of evolution has become an indispensable dogmatic belief. These circles are stubbornly attached to materialist philosophy and are influenced by Darwinism as the only materialist explanation of nature.

They sometimes openly admit this. Richard Lewontin, a famous geneticist from Harvard University and at the same time a foremost evolutionist admits that he is "first a materialist, then a scientist" in these words:

> It is not that the methods and institutions of science somehow compel us accept a material explanation of the phenomenal world, but, on the contrary, **that we are forced by our *a priori* adherence to material causes to create an apparatus of investigation and a set of concepts that produce material explanations, no matter how counter-intuitive, no matter how mystifying to the uninitiated. Moreover, that materialism is absolute, so we cannot allow a Divine Foot in the door.**[155]

These words are a clear statement that Darwinism is a dogma kept alive for the sake of attachment to materialist philosophy. This dogma considers that nothing exists but matter. For this reason it believes that non-living, unconscious matter created life. It accepts that millions of living species, for example birds, fish, giraffes, tigers, insects, trees, flowers, whales, and human beings emerged from effects which went on within innate matter, in other words rain and lightning. This is really a belief contrary to both intelligence and science. But Darwinists continue to defend this belief in order "not to allow a Divine Foot in the door."

Everyone who does not look at the origin of living things with a materialist prejudice will perceive this clear truth: All living things are the work of a Creator which possesses a superior power, knowledge, and intelligence. The Creator is God, Who created the whole universe out of nothing, who designed it in the most perfect manner and created and gave form to all living things.

NOTES

1   Robert Wright, *The Moral Animal*, Vintage Books, New York: 1994, p.7

2   Anton Pannekoek, *Marxism and Darwinism*, Translated by Nathan Weiser, Chicago, Charles H. Kerr &Company, 1912, http://csf.colorado.edu/psn/ marx/Other/ Pannekoek/Archive/1912-Darwin/

3   Theodore D. Hall, *The Scientific Background of the Nazi "Race Purification" Program*, http://www.trufax.org/ avoid/nazi.html

4   Francis Darwin, *The Life and Letters of Charles Darwin*, D. Appleton and Co., 1896, vol. 2, p.294

5   Stephen Jay Gould, *The Mismeasure of Man*, W.W. Norton and Company, New York, 1981, p. 72

6   Jacques Barzun, *Darwin, Marx, Wagner*, Garden City, N.Y.: Doubleday, 1958, pp.94-95, cited in Henry M. Morris, *The Long war Against God*, Baker Book House, 1989, p. 70

7   A.E. Wilder-Smith, *Man's Origin Man's Destiny*, The Word for Today Publishing, 1993, p.166

8   Charles Darwin, *The Descent of Man*, 2nd edition, New York, A L. Burt Co., 1874, p. 178

9   Charles Darwin, *The Descent of Man*, 2nd edition, New York, A L. Burt Co., 1874, p. 171

10   Godfrey Lienhardt, *Social Anthropology*, Oxford University Press, p. 11

11   Benjamin Farrington, *What Darwin Really Said*, London: Sphere Books, 1971, pp. 54-56

12   James Ferguson, "The Laboratory of Racism", *New Scientist*, vol. 103, (September 1984, p. 18)

13   Lalita Prasad Vidyarthi, *Racism, Science and Pseudo-Science*, Unesco, France, Vendôme, 1983. p. 54

14   David N. Menton, Ph.D., The Religion of Nature: Social Darwinism, *St. Louis MetroVoice*, September 1994, Vol. 4, No. 9

15   Stephen Jay Gould, *Ever Since Darwin*, W. W. Norton & Company, New York 1992, p. 217

16   Stephen Jay Gould, *Ever Since Darwin*, W. W. Norton & Company, New York 1992, p. 220

17   Alaeddin Şenel, *Irk ve Irkçılık Düşüncesi* (The Idea of Race and Racism), Ankara: Bilim ve Sanat Yayınları, 1993, p. 67-68

18   Thomas Gossett, *Race: The History of an Idea in America*, Dallas: Southern Methodist University Press, 1963, p.81 cited in Alaeddin Şenel, *Irk ve Irkçılık Düşüncesi* (The Idea of Race and Racism), Ankara:Bilim ve Sanat Yayınları, 1993, p. 68

19   Jacques Attali, *1492*, Librairie Arthème Fayard, 1991, p.197

20   François de Fontette, *Le Racisme* (Racism), 6th ed. Presses Universitaires de France, 1988, p. 40-41

21   James Joll, *Europe Since 1870: An International History*, Penguin Books, Middlesex, 1990, p. 102-103

22   Kenneth J. Hsü., reply to comment on "Darwin's Three Mistakes", *Geology*, vol. 15, April 1987, p. 377

23   Süleyman Kocabaş, *Hindistan Yolu ve Petrol Uğruna Yapılanlar: Türkiye ve İngiltere* (The Road to India and What Has Been Done for the Sake of Oil: Turkey and Britain), 1.baskı, İstanbul: Vatan Yayınları, 1985, p. 231

24   Francis Darwin, *The Life and Letters of Charles Darwin*, Vol.I, 1888. New York D. Appleton and Company, p.285-286

25   Henry M. Morris, *The Long War Against God*, Baker Book House, 1989, p. 70

26   Henry M. Morris, *The Long War Against God*, Baker Book House, 1989, p. 71

27   Thomas Gossett, *Race: The History of an Idea in America*, Dallas: Southern Methodist University Press, 1963, p.188

28   Alaeddin Şenel, *Irk ve Irkçılık Düşüncesi* (The Idea of

Race and Racism), Ankara:Bilim ve Sanat Yayınları, 1993, p. 85-90

29   Henry Fairfield Osborn, "The Evolution of Human Races", *Natural History*, April 1980, p. 129 – reprinted from January/February 1926 issue

30- François de Fontette, *Le Racisme* (Racism), 6th ed. Presses Universitaires de France, 1988, p. 101

31   François de Fontette, *Le Racisme* (Racism), 6th ed. Presses Universitaires de France, 1988, p. 105

32   Jani Roberts, *How New-Darwinism Justified Taking Land From Aborigines and Murdering Them in Australia*, http://www.gn.apc.org/inquirer/ausrace.html

33   Jani Roberts, *How New-Darwinism Justified Taking Land From Aborigines and Murdering Them in Australia*, http://www.gn.apc.org/inquirer/ausrace.html

34   Jani Robert, *How New-Darwinism Justified Taking Land From Aborigines and Murdering Them in Australia*, http://www.gn.apc.org/inquirer/ausrace.html

35   *Creation Ex Nihilo*, Vol 14, No. 2, March-May 1992, p. 17

36   *Philadelphia Daily News*, 28 April 1997

37   Philips Verner Bradford, Harvey Blume, *Ota Benga, The Pygmy in the Zoo*, Canada, October 1993 p. 269

38   Philips Verner Bradford, Harvey Blume, *Ota Benga, The Pygmy in the Zoo*, Canada, October 1993, p. 267

39   Philips Verner Bradford, Harvey Blume, *Ota Benga, The Pygmy in the Zoo*, Canada, October 1993, p. 266

40   Philips Verner Bradford, Harvey Blume, *Ota Benga, The Pygmy in the Zoo*, Canada, October 1993, p.264

41   Philips Verner Bradford, Harvey Blume, *Ota Benga, The Pygmy in the Zoo*, Canada, October 1993, p. 259

42   Bryan Appleyard, *Brave New Worlds*, Harper Collins Publishers, London 1999, p. 49-50

43   Alaeddin Şenel, *Irk ve Irkçılık Düşüncesi* (The Idea of Race and Racism), Ankara:Bilim ve Sanat Yayınları, 1993, pp.62-6

44   *War Against Religion* http://www.geocities.com/ Heartland/Meadows/1733/book2-ch3.html

45   J. Tenenbaum., *Race and Reich*, Twayne Pub., New York, p. 211, 1956; cited by Jerry Bergman, Darwinism and the Nazi Race Holocaust, http://www.trueorigin.org/holocaust.htm

46   L.H. Gann, "Adolf Hitler, The Complete Totalitarian", *The Intercollegiate Review*, Fall 1985, p. 24; cited in Henry M. Morris, *The Long war Against God*, Baker Book House, 1989, p. 78

47   K. Ludmerer., *Eugenics, In: Encyclopedia of Bioethics*, Edited by Mark Lappe, The Free Press, New York, p. 457, 1978; cited by Jerry Bergman, Darwinism and the Nazi Race Holocaust, www.trueorigin.org/ holocaust.htm

48   G. Stein., Biological science and the roots of Nazism, *American Scientist* 76(1):p. 54, 1988; cited by Jerry Bergman, Darwinism and the Nazi Race Holocaust, http://www.trueorigin.org/holocaust.htm

49   Adolf Hitler, *Mein Kampf*, München: Verlag Franz Eher Nachfolger, 1993, p. 44, 447-448; cited by A.E. Wilder Smith, Man's Origin Man's Destiny, The Word For Today Publishing 1993, p. 163, 164

50   P. Weindling, *Health, Race and German Policies Between National Unification and Nazism 1870-1945*, Cambridge University Press, Cambridge, MA, 1989, cited by Jerry Bergman, *Darwinism and The Nazi Race Holocaust*, www.trueorigin.org/holocaust.htm

51   Theodore D. Hall, *The Scientific Background of the Nazi "Race Purification" Program*, http://www.trufax.org/ avoid/nazi.html

52   Theodore D. Hall, *The Scientific Background of the Nazi "Race Purification" Program*, http://www.trufax.org/ avoid/nazi.html

53 John J. Michalczyk (editor), *Nazi Medicine: In The Shadow of The Reich* (documentary film), First Run Features, New York, 1997

54 George J. Stein, "Biological Science and the Roots of Nazism", *American Scientist*, vol. 76, (January/February 1988), p. 52

55 Sir Arthur Keith, *Evolution and Ethics*, New York: G.P. Putnam's Sons, 1947, p. 14

56 Robert Clark, *Darwin: Before and After*, Grand Rapids International Press, Grand Rapids, MI, 1958. p.115

57 A. Keith, *Evolution and Ethics*, G. P. Putnam's Sons, New York, p. 230, 1946, cited by Jerry Bergman, *Darwinism and the Nazi Race Holocaust*, www.trueorigin.org/holocaust.htm

58 Francis Schaeffer, *How Shall We Then Live?*, Old Tappan, N.J.: Revell, 1976, p. 151; cited in Henry M. Morris, *The Long war Against God*, Baker Book House, 1989, p. 78

59 A. Hitler, Hitler's Secret Conversations 1941–1944, With an introductory essay on The Mind of Adolf Hitler by H.R. Trevor-Roper, Farrar, Straus and Young, New York, p. 117, 1953; cited by Jerry Bergman, *Darwinism and the Nazi Race Holocaust*, http://www.trueorigin.org/holocaust.htm

60 Daniel Gasman, *The Scientific Origins of National Socialism: Social Darwinism in Earnest Haeckel and the German Monist League*, New York: American Elsevier Press, 1971, p. 168

61 Robert E.D. Clark, *Darwin: Before and After*, London: Paternoster Press, 1948, p. 115, cited in Henry M. Morris, *The Long War Against God*, Baker Book House, 1989, p. 81

62 Denis Mack Smith, *Mussolini*, p. 14

63 John P. Diggins, *Mussolini and Fascism*, Princeton University Press, 1972, p. 15

64 *Çağdaş Liderler Ansiklopedisi* (The Encyclopaedia of Contemporary Leaders), Vol. 2, p. 669

65 James Joll, *Europe Since 1870: An International History*, Penguin Books, Middlesex, 1990, p. 164

66 M.F. Ashley-Montagu, *Man in Process* (New York: World. Pub. Co. 1961) pp. 76, 77 cited in Bolton Davidheiser, W E Lammers (ed) Scientific Studies in Special Creationism, 1971, p. 338-339

67 A.E. Wiggam, *The New Dialogue of Science*, Garden Publishing Co., Garden City, NY, p. 102, 1922; cited by Jerry Bergman, *Darwinism and the Nazi Race Holocaust*, http://www.trueorigin.org/holocaust.htm

68 Robert Clark, *Darwin: Before and After*, Grand Rapids International Press, Grand Rapids, MI, 1958., s. 115-116; cited by Jerry Bergman, *Darwinism and the Nazi Race Holocaust*, http://www.trueorigin.org/holocaust.htm

69 Jerry Bergman, *Darwinism and the Nazi Race Holocaust*, http://www.trueorigin.org/holocaust.htm

70 Earnest Haeckel, *The History of Creation: Or the Development of the Earth and Its Inhabitants by the Action of Natural Causes*, Appleton, New York, 1876, p. 170; cited by Jerry Bergman, *Darwinism and the Nazi Race Holocaust*, http://www.trueorigin.org/holocaust. htm

71 Theodore D. Hall, *The Scientific Background of the Nazi "Race Purification" Program*, http://www.trufax.org/avoid/nazi.html

72 Marshall Hall, *Hitler, Lenin, Stalin, Mao et al: The Role of Darwinian Evolutionism in Their Lives*, http://www.fixedearth.com/hlsm.html

73 Max Nordau, The Philosophy and Morals of War, *North American Review* 169 (1889):794 cited in Richard Hofstadter, *Social Darwinism in American Thought*, Boston: Beacon Press, 1955, p.171)

74 *Tempo* Magazine, 14 July 1991

75 http://chefsseite.tsx.org/

76 *Sabah* Daily, 12 August 2000

77 *San Francisco Examiner*, 1 April 1997

78 Conway Zirkle, *Evolution, Marxian Biology and the Social Scene*, Philadelphia: University of Pennsylvania Press, 1959, pp. 85-87

79 Conway Zirkle, *Evolution, Marxian Biology and the Social Scene*, Philadelphia: University of Pennsylvania Press, 1959, pp. 85-87

80 Conway Zirkle, *Evolution, Marxian Biology and the Social Scene*, Philadelphia: University of Pennsylvania Press, 1959, pp. 85-87

81 Stephen Jay Gould, *Ever Since Darwin*, W. W. Norton & Company, New York 1992, p. 26

82 Friedrich Engels, *Socialism: Utopian and Scientific*, Foreign Languages Press, Peking 1975, p. 67

83 Gertrude Himmelfarb, *Darwin and the Darwinian Revolution*, London: Chatto & Windus, 1959, pp. 348-9

84 Friedrich Engels, *Socialism: Utopian and Scientific*, Foreign Languages Press, Peking 1975, p. 67

85 Conway Zirkle, *Evolution, Marxian Biology and the Social Scene*, (University of Pennsylvania Press, 1959), pp.85-86

86 Tom Bethell, "Burning Darwin to Save Marx", *Harper's Magazine*, (December 1978), p.37

87 *Karl Marx Biyografi* (The Biography of Karl Marx), Öncü Yayınevi, p. 368

88 John N. Moore, *The Impact of Evolution on the Social Sciences*, Impact No. 52, www.icr.org/pubs/imp/imp-052.htm

89 Marshall Hall, *Hitler, Lenin, Stalin, Mao et al: The Role of Darwinian Evolutionism in Their Lives*, http://www.fixedearth.com/hlsm.html

90- Alan Woods and Ted Grant, *Reason in Revolt: Marxism and Modern Science*, London:1993

91- Kent Hovind, *The False Religion of Evolution*, http://www.royalse.com/scroll/evolve/ndxng.html

92- E. Yaroslavsky, *Landmarks in the Life of Stalin*, Moscow: Foreign Languages Publishing House, 1940, pp. 8.; cited by Paul G. Humber, *Stalin's Brutal Faith*, Vital articles on Science/Creation October 1987, Impact No. 172

93 E. Yaroslavsky, *Landmarks in the Life of Stalin*, Moscow: Foreign Languages Publishing House, 1940, pp. 8.; cited by Paul G. Humber, *Stalin's Brutal Faith*, Vital articles on Science/Creation October 1987, Impact No. 172

94 K. Mehnert, *Kampf um Mao's Erbe*, Deutsche Verlags-Anstalt, 1977

95 Marshall Hall, *Hitler, Lenin, Stalin, Mao et al: The Role of Darwinian Evolutionism in Their Lives*, http://www.fixedearth.com/hlsm.html

96 Robert Milner, *Encyclopaedia of Evolution* 1990 p.81

97 Michael Ruse: The Long March of Darwin, *New Scientist* 103, August 16, 1984: 35; cited in Henry M. Morris, *The Long war Against God*, Baker Book House, 1989, pp.85-86

98 David Jorafsky, *Soviet Marxism and Natural Science*, New York: Columbia University Press, 1961, p.4

99 Nicolas Werth, "Le Pouvoir soviétique et l'Eglise orthodoxe de la collectivisation à la Constitution de 1936", Revue d'études comparatives Est-Quest nos. 3-4, 1993, pp.41-49 cited by Stéphane Courtois, Nicolas Werth, Jean-Louis Panné, Andrzej Paczkowski, Karel Bartosek, Jean-Louis Margolin, *The Black Book of Communism*, Harvard University Press, 1999, p. 172

100 Samuel T. Francis, *The Soviet Strategy of Terror*, The Heritage Foundation, 1981, p. 46

101 V. I. Lenin; *Collected Works*, 4th English Edition, Progress Publishers, Moscow, 1964, p. 180

102 V. I. Lenin, *The Proletarian Revolution and The Renegade Kautsky* (Moscow: Foreign Languages Publishing House, 1952, pp. 32-33, 20)

103 V. I. Lenin, *Collected Works*, Moscow, Volume 35, p. 238

104 V. I. Lenin, Collected Works, Vol. 24, pp. 38-41, Progress Publishers, Moscow, 1964.

105 V.I. Lenin, Polnoe sobranie sochinenii, (Complete Collected Works), Moscow, Gos.-izd-vo polit. Lit-ry, 1958-1966, 35: 311, cited by Stéphane Courtois, Nicolas Werth, Jean-Louis Panné, Andrzej Paczkowski, Karel Bartosek, Jean-Louis Margolin, *The Black Book of Communism*, Harvard University Press, 1999, p. 59

106 Ann Arbor, Leon Troçki, *Terrorism or Communism*, University of Michigan Press, 1961, p. 58

107 Protokoly zasedanii VSIK 4-sozyva, Stenograficheskii otchet (Protocols of the sessions of the CEC in the fourth phase: Stenographic account) (Moscow, 1918), p. 250

108 Harrison E. Salisbury, "Reading The Gulag Archipelago is like no other reading experience of our day," Book-of-the-Month Club NEWS, Midsummer, 1974, pp. 4,5.

109 Russian Center for the Conservation and Study of Historic Documents, Moscow, 17/84/75/59, cited by Stéphane Courtois, Nicolas Werth, Jean-Louis Panné, Andrzej Paczkowski, Karel Bartosek, Jean-Louis Margolin, *The Black Book of Communism*, Harvard University Press, 1999, p. 100

110 Quoted in V.I. Brovkin, *Behind the Front Lines of the Civil War: Political Parties and Social Movements in Russia, 1918-1922*, Princeton: Princeton University Press, 1981, p. 353, cited by Stéphane Courtois, Nicolas Werth, Jean-Louis Panné, Andrzej Paczkowski, Karel Bartosek, Jean-Louis Margolin, *The Black Book of Communism*, Harvard University Press, 1999, p. 101

111 *Krasnyi Mech*, no.1 (18 August 1919), p.1 cited by Stéphane Courtois, Nicolas Werth, Jean-Louis Panné, Andrzej Paczkowski, Karel Bartosek, Jean-Louis Margolin, *The Black Book of Communism*, Harvard University Press, 1999, p. 102

112 Stéphane Courtois, Nicolas Werth, Jean-Louis Panné, Andrzej Paczkowski, Karel Bartosek, Jean-Louis Margolin, *The Black Book of Communism*, Harvard University Press, 1999, p. 119

113 Quoted in Julian Gorkin, *Les Communistes contre la révolution espagnole*, Paris: Belfond, 1978, p.181, cited by Stéphane Courtois, Nicolas Werth, Jean-Louis Panné, Andrzej Paczkowski, Karel Bartosek, Jean-Louis Margolin, *The Black Book of Communism*, Harvard University Press, 1999, p. 342

114 Stéphane Courtois, Nicolas Werth, Jean-Louis Panné, Andrzej Paczkowski, Karel Bartosek, Jean-Louis Margolin, *The Black Book of Communism*, Harvard University Press, 1999, p. 29

115 Stéphane Courtois, Nicolas Werth, Jean-Louis Panné, Andrzej Paczkowski, Karel Bartosek, Jean-Louis Margolin, *The Black Book of Communism*, Harvard University Press, 1999, p. 470-471

116 Stéphane Courtois, Nicolas Werth, Jean-Louis Panné, Andrzej Paczkowski, Karel Bartosek, Jean-Louis Margolin, *The Black Book of Communism*, Harvard University Press, 1999, p. 4

117 P.J. Darlington, *Evolution for Naturalists*, 1980, s. 243-244

118 Edward E. Ericson, Jr., "Solzhenitsyn - Voice from the Gulag", *Eternity*, October 1985, pp. 23, 24.

119 Alaeddin Şenel, *Irk ve Irkçılık Düşüncesi* (The Idea of Race and Racism), Ankara: Belem ve Sanat Yayınları, 1993, p. 61

120 Herbert Spencer, *Social Status*, 1850, p. 414-415

121 The Challenge of Facts and Other Essays, as quoted in Mason Drukman, *Community and Purpose in America: An Analysis of American Political Theory*, New York: McGraw-Hill, 1971, p. 202.

122 R. Milner, *Encyclopedia of Evolution* 1990 p. 412

123 Thomas F. Gossett, *Race: The History of an Idea in America*, Dallas: Southern Methodist University Press, 1963, p. 170

124 Chauncey Depew, *My Memories of Eighty Years*, New York, 1922, pp.383-384

125 James J. Hill, *Highways of Progress*, New York, 1910, pp. 126, 137

126 Andrew Carnegie, Autobiography, Boston 1920, p. 327, cited in Richard Hofstadter, *Social Darwinism in American Thought*, Boston: Beacon Press, 1955, p. 45

127 Andrew Carnegie, Wealth, North American Review 148, 1889, s. 655-657, cited in Richard Hofstadter, *Social Darwinism in American Thought*, Boston: Beacon Press, 1955, pp. 45-46

128 Kenneth J. Hsü, "Darwin's Three Mistakes", *Geology*, vol.14, June 1986, p. 534

129 Bolton Davidheiser, W E Lemmerts (ed) *Scientific Studies in Special Creationism*, 1971 p. 338-339.

130 H. Enoch, *Evolution or Creation*, 1966 p.145

131 Ernst Mayr, "Interview", Omni, March/April 1988, p. 46; cited in Henry M. Morris, John D. Morris, *The Modern Creation Triology*, Vol. 3, p. 12

132 Kenneth A. Ham, *The Lie Evolution*, Master Books, April 1997, p. 84

133 Theodosius Dobzhansky, "Ethics and Values in Biological and Cultural Evolution", *Zygon, the Journal of Religion and Science*, as reported in Los Angeles Times, part IV (June 16, 1974), p. 6

134 Stephen Jay Gould, *Ever Since Darwin*, W. W. Norton & Company, New York 1992, p. 223

135 Richard Dawkins, *Unweaving The Rainbow*, Houghton Mifflin Company, Newyork, 1998, p. ix)

136 Earthwatch, March 1989, p. 17; cited in Henry M. Morris, *The Long War Against God*, Baker Book House, 1989, p. 57

137 Sidney Fox, Klaus Dose, *Molecular Evolution and The Origin of Life*, New York: Marcel Dekker, 1977. p. 2

138 Alexander I. Oparin, *Origin of Life*, (1936) New York, Dover Publications, 1953 (Reprint), p.196

139 "New Evidence on Evolution of Early Atmosphere and Life", *Bulletin of the American Meteorological Society*, vol 63, November 1982, p. 1328-1330.

140 Stanley Miller, *Molecular Evolution of Life: Current Status of the Prebiotic Synthesis of Small Molecules*, 1986, p. 7

141 Jeffrey Bada, *Earth*, February 1998, v. 40

142 Leslie E. Orgel, The Origin of Life on Earth, *Scientific American*, vol 271, October 1994, p. 78

143 Charles Darwin, *The Origin of Species*: A Facsimile of the First Edition, Harvard University Press, 1964, p. 189

144 Charles Darwin, *The Origin of Species*: A Facsimile of the First Edition, Harvard University Press, 1964, p. 184.

145 B. G. Ranganathan, *Origins?*, Pennsylvania: The Banner Of Truth Trust, 1988.

146 Charles Darwin, *The Origin of Species: A Facsimile of the First Editio*n, Harvard University Press, 1964, p. 179

147 Derek A. Ager, "The Nature of the Fossil Record", *Proceedings of the British Geological Association*, vol 87, 1976, p. 133

148 Douglas J. Futuyma, *Science on Trial*, New York: Pantheon Books, 1983. p. 197

149 Solly Zuckerman, *Beyond The Ivory Tower*, New York: Toplinger Publications, 1970, ss. 75-94; Charles E. Oxnard, "The Place of Australopithecines in Human Evolution: Grounds for Doubt", Nature, vol 258, p. 389

150 J. Rennie, "Darwin's Current Bulldog: Ernst Mayr", *Scientific American*, December 1992

151 Alan Walker, *Science*, vol. 207, 1980, p. 1103; A. J. Kelso, Physical Antropology, 1st ed., New York: J. B. Lipincott Co., 1970, s. 221; M. D. Leakey, Olduvai Gorge, vol. 3, Cambridge: Cambridge University Press, 1971, p. 272

152 *Time*, November 1996

153 S. J. Gould, *Natural History*, vol. 85, 1976, p. 30

154 Solly Zuckerman, *Beyond The Ivory Tower*, New York: Toplinger Publications, 1970, p. 19

155 Richard Lewontin, "The Demon-Haunted World", *The New York Review of Books*, 9 January, 1997, p. 28.

ALSO BY HARUN YAHYA

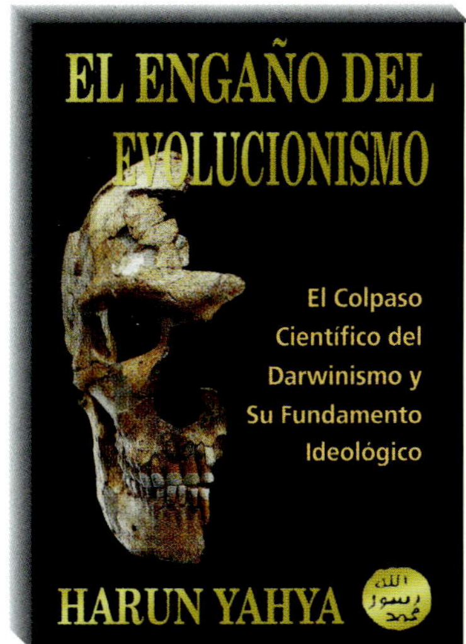

Many people think that Darwin's Theory of Evolution is a proven fact. Contrary to this conventional wisdom, recent developments in science completely disprove the theory. The only reason Darwinism is still foisted on people by means of a worldwide propaganda campaign lies in the ideological aspects of the theory. All secular ideologies and philosophies try to provide a basis for themselves by relying on the theory of evolution.

This book clarifies the scientific collapse of the theory of evolution in a way that is detailed but easy to understand. It reveals the frauds and distortions committed by evolutionists to "prove" evolution. Finally it analyzes the powers and motives that strive to keep this theory alive and make people believe in it.

Anyone who wants to learn about the origin of living things, including mankind, needs to read this book.

238 PAGES WITH 166 PICTURES IN COLOUR

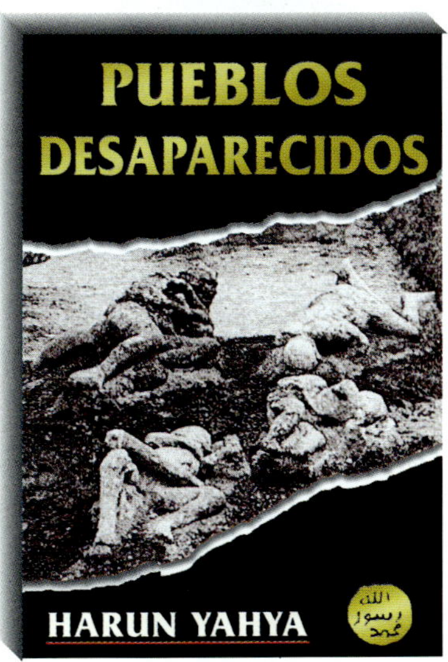

Many societies that rebelled against the will of Allah or regarded His messengers as enemies were wiped off the face of the earth completely... All of them were destroyed— some by a volcanic eruption, some by a disastrous flood, and some by a sand storm... Perished Nations examines these penalties as revealed in the verses of the Quran and in light of archaeological discoveries.

149 PAGES WITH 73 PICTURES IN COLOUR

The purpose of this book is to warn people against the day on which they will say "If only we did not rebel against Allah. If only we listened to the messengers…" and therefore feel deep regret. This is a summons to live for the cause of Allah when there is still time.

88 PAGES

Fourteen centuries ago, God (Allah) revealed the Qur'an, the guide to truth for mankind, and summoned all humanity to seek salvation by following the commandments of this Book. From the day it was first revealed until Judgement Day, this final holy Book will remain the sole guide for humanity. The unprecedented style and the superior wisdom inherent in the Qur'an is conclusive evidence confirming that it is the Word of Allah. Apart from this, there are a number of miracles verifying the fact that the Qur'an is the revelation of Allah, one of them being that, 1,400 years ago, it declared a number of scientific facts that have only been established thanks to the technological breakthroughs of the 20th century. In this book, in addition to the scientific miracles of the Qur'an, you will also find messages regarding the future and examples of its "mathematical miracle."

120 PAGES WITH 73 PİCTURES IN COLOUR

Ruling over the world of science in the 19th century, the materialist philosophy had proposed that the universe is an uncontrolled heap of matter that existed since eternity. The discoveries made in the twentieth century, however, entirely refuted this materialist claim. Today, science has proven that the universe was created from nothing with a Big Bang. Moreover, all physical balances of the universe are designed to support human life. Everything from the nuclear reactions in stars to the chemical properties of a carbon atom or a water molecule, is created in a glorious harmony.

This is the exalted and flawless creation of Allah, the Lord of All the Worlds.

The Creation of the Universe will soon be available also in French and Spanish.

192 PAGES WITH 91 PICTURES IN COLOUR

They said 'Glory be to You!
We have no knowledge except what
You have taught us.
You are the All-Knowing, the All-Wise.'
(Surat al-Baqara: 32)